José Antonio Burciaga's

Drink Cultura

Chicanismo

"Burciaga's splendid wit and humor are the genuine article, *la mera cosa,* a true reflection of the sometimes poignant, oftentimes absurd life of the Chicano in America."
—Luis Valdez

"A friendly but always informative collection of commentary on *Chicanismo,* Mexican history, language, the author's family and hometown El Paso, the *movimento* of the 1960s and 1970s. Burciaga's writing is brisk and the subjects sweeping but never facile. Our young people need to hear his voice and the older generation needs to remember the causes for our uproar."
—Gary Soto

"Burciaga has a gift for striking the Chicano funny bone every time. He is literate without being pompous, political without being an idealogue, playful without being frivolous. He is a true comic because he knowns that we laugh the hardest when we are in pain. I can think of no other writer from his background who is so in tune with the socio-political humor of the North American Hispanic world and who can write about it with such authenticity."
—Arturo Islas

About The Author Of This Book

José Antonio Burciaga is a Resident Fellow, artist and writer at Stanford University. Raised in the West Texas border town of El Paso, he is a seasoned Chicano cultural activist, muralist, humorist and founding member of the comedy group *Culture Clash*. His book *Undocumented Love* (Chusma House) won the Before Columbus American Book Award for poetry in 1981.

Drink Cultura

Drink Cultura

Chicanismo

José Antonio Burciaga

JOSHUA ODELL EDITIONS   CAPRA PRESS SANTA BARBARA   1993

Acknowledgments

The essays in this collection originally appeared in the following publications, to whose editors and publishers thanks are due.

"Reasons to Celebrate *El Cinco de Mayo*," *Hispanic Link News Service,* May 1981.
"Ernesto Galarza," *Hispanic Link News Service,* July 1984.
"Last Supper of Chicano Heroes," *Los Angeles Times,* May 3, 1988.
"La Cate," *Hispanic Link News Service,* November, 1990.
"Tiburcio Vásquez: A Chicano Perspective," *The Californians,*
    May 1985,Vol. 3, No. 3.
"Late Night Memories of Ciudad Juarez," *Hispanic Magazine,* August 1989.
"The Great Taco War," *Peninsula Times Tribune,* November 13, 1991.
"Childhood, Imagination and the Art Process," The Fourth R: Art, Auphrat
    Gallery, De Anza College, Cupertino, CA, January 1992.
"Mixed Tex-Cal Marriage," *Hispanic Link News Service,* February 1985.
"My Ecumenical Father," *Vista Magazine,* December 1986

LIBRARY OF CONGRESS CATALOGING-IN-PUBLICATION DATA

Burciaga, José Antonio.
    Drink Cultura : Chicanismo / José Antonio Burciaga.
        p.   cm.
    ISBN 1-877741-07-8 : $10.95
    1. Hispanic Americans—Social life and customs.   I. Title.
E184.S75B85   1992
305.868'72073—dc20   92-32614
                                                                       CIP

BOOK DESIGN BY ALBERT CHIANG
TYPESETTING BY PAGINATION STATION
PRINTED IN THE UNITED STATES OF AMERICA
FIRST EDITION
5 4 3 2 1

For

Cecilia,
my children
Rebeca y Toño

their grandparents
Rebeca & Bernardino Preciado

in memory of my parents
José Cruz & María Guadalupe Burciaga

and to my extended familia
my carnales Pifas, Rulis, Big Norm, Clete,
Joe; mis hermanas, Lupe, Margie, Connie, Marty;
and my sobrinos, Cathy, Patricia, Aaron,
Oscar, Michael and Marisa

Contents

"The greatest distance between people is not space but culture."

JAMAKE HIGHWATER

Chief *Wachuseh*

I first heard the word *wachuseh* before I started school and learned English. For me, the word had always been Spanish. "This is better than wachuseh," my father would say in Spanish and I would be impressed because he reserved the word for only the best. He never told me what it meant, but I knew. Wachuseh was a mythical Indian chief, perhaps an Aztec emperor, or at least the Indian chief on the red covers of school writing tablets. I could visualize him, tall, muscular, toasted brown with an Aztec feathered head dress, the epitome of perfection.

Eventually, I came to decode and recognize that wachuseh came from the question "What did you say?" But by then the four-word question had become so engraved in

3

my mind that to this day, an Indian chief comes to mind when I hear it. Wachuseh became a word meaning something that was better than anything anyone could say.

Wachuseh has been a common and popular phrase among immigrants to this country. It's often used as a question when someone doesn't understand English or the concept of what is being said in English. The phrase may have originated from English speakers who could not understand the accented speech of an immigrant. It's also popular among many Afro-Americans and effectively expressed as "whachusay?" when questioning or disbelieving a statement.

I love words such as wachuseh as much as the people who use them. The significance of such compressed words goes beyond their original meaning to say even more. Born into a bicultural and bilingual world, I have experienced the birth of new words, new worlds, ideas that came from two languages and two cultures, words that changed meanings and power. So many other cultures and languages from Black English to Yiddish have contributed to the evolution and enrichment of the English language. These words enriched because they gave birth to a new world of ideas from a combination of cultures, ideas that were lacking a name until then.

Chutzpah filled a void in the English language; there was nothing in our slang like it. The introduction of *macho* into the English language was another such idea, even though the English definition has a more negative connotation than the Spanish, where the term can be as innocent as its basic literal definition of "male." In Mexican Spanish it's *huevos,* in peninsular Spanish it's *cojones* for "balls." Some Mexican or Chicano ideas have no English

4

words. To call someone a *pendejo* in Spanish is not the same as calling him or her stupid or even *estúpido* or *estúpida.*

My father had a vocabulary of Spanish words that to this day are not found in popular Spanish language dictionaries. He was born into a poor, migrant farm working family in a community of people that still used ancient words that some found improper and backwards but are to be found in Miguel Cervantez's classic *Don Quixote.* My father commonly used words such as *minjurne* for mixture, or *cachibaches* for junk. I would hear them without knowing their definition but I knew exactly what he meant when talking within a specific context. Some words were archaic, others were a combination of English and Spanish. And though he knew the "standard" Spanish of "educated" people, he also worked, lived, laughed and cried with words that were more expressive and indigenous to the border than standard Spanish.

Drink Cultura is a collection of stories and commentaries about what you say, about what they said, about what my father said, about what I say, about what I've heard said—going beyond the question and shooting it back as wachuseh. The ironies in the experience of living within, between and sometimes outside of two cultures; the damnation and the salvation, the celebration of it all.

Con Safos

C/s

At one time or another many of us have seen the c/s sign-off on Chicano *placas* and graffitti in the Southwest or Midwest. It's a very common Chicano symbol but its true origin and significance is nebulous.

It is not a Mexican symbol but a Chicano, a Mexican-American, symbol. Its origin is unknown but, like the *Pachuco,* it probably originated in South El Paso's *Segundo Barrio.* The c/s sign-off means *con safos*, and translates literally as "with safety." It was meant as a safety precaution, a barrio copyright, patent pending. No one else could use or dishonor the grafitti. It was an honorable code of conduct, a literary imprimatur. Like saying "amen," it ended discussion. Above all, it meant, "anything you say against me will bounce back to you." Most kids respected a placa if signed off with the c/s. Without that symbol, a placa would sooner or later get scribbled on or erased. Some kids would put a double c/s sign or put xxx after it, or a skull and cross bones, which physically threatened anyone who did not honor and respect the code.

A precise definition for con safos or safos is lacking because it comes from *Caló,* the Chicano dialect. Caló originally defined the Spanish gypsy dialect. But Chicano Caló is the combination of a few basic influences: Hispanicized English; Anglicized Spanish; and the use of archaic 15th-century Spanish words such as *truje* for *traer* (to bring), or *haiga,* for *haya* from *haber* (to have). These words were left in isolated pockets of Northern Mexico and the Southwest, especially New Mexico, by *conquistadores españoles.* In this country, Caló is not recognized as a dialect but is derisively called Tex-Mex, or Spanglish, without taking into consideration its unique multicultural, political, societal and linguistic function and formation.

Returning to con safos, the closest possible Spanish word from which safos could have come would be *safó* from *safar,* or *safado,* which translates to slip or slipped. This is a plausible definition since the c/s is meant to let insults slip off, to protect and shield from attacks. In a game of marbles, Chicano kids used the word *safis* if they let the marble slip before shooting it in the right direction. By saying safis the marble shooter was allowed to try again.

Some Chicanos will also end a placa, graffitti, with the message *con o sin safos,* which means that with or without safety, with or without this code, whether you like it or not, whether you insult me back or not, this placa, insult or praise, stands.

Nowadays there is also a con safos hand sign that is rarely, if ever, used. It entails a raised hand, palm open towards your opponent but with the fingers bent down over the top of the palm to act as a shield and deflect any insults back to the perpetrator. This was primarily and most effectively used against "finger throwing" and it had as much validity and effect as any spoken insult.

Chicano artists and writers of the late sixties and early seventies often used the c/s symbol in signing their works, especially when the works were political or cultural in nature. There was even a magazine entitled *Con Safos.*

In these short pieces, my ending logo is the c/s sign, like an amen. Whether you agree with me or not, whether you like it or not, with all due respect, this is my reality.

$$C/s$$

Pendejismo

Most popular Mexican cuss words begin
with a "p." Why words such as *pinchi, puto, político* and
pendejo, carry such a harsh negative sound, I don't know.
I'm not a linguist.

Pinchi, or *pinche,* is used to describe someone who is
mean-spirited. The degree of insult depends on the inten-
sity, the context, and who is delivering it. I don't know why
the word is considered vulgar. In Spain, a pinche is a
kitchen helper, and a few restaurants are named El
Pinche, which many Mexican and Chicano tourists find
hilarious.

Once when I was a kid, my big sister was angry and
wanted to pinch me, so I said, "¡No pinching!" She ran to
Mom and said, "¡Mamá! ¡Antonio called me a pinchi!"

Well, Mother, proper and educated woman that she was, gave me a tongue-lashing that I never forgot, and I could never convince her or my sister that what I had said was "No pinching!" To this day, my sister will only laugh and say she doesn't remember anything, but my ears still sting.

A *puta* is a whore in vulgar Spanish, as opposed to *prostituta* for prostitute. A *puto* is a homosexual.

Pendejo is probably the least offensive of these P words. In Guadalajara and some other parts of Mexico, it is a common everyday word. For the non-Spanish speaking, the word is pronounced pen-deh-ho (not pen-day-hoe); feminine, pen-deh-ha; plural pendejas or pendejos. The noun, or committed act of a pendejo*(a),* is a *pendejada.* The verb is to *pendejear.* The term pendejo is commonly used outside of polite conversation and basically describes someone who is stupid or does something stupid. It's much stronger to call someone a pendejo than the standard Spanish *estúpido* But be careful when calling someone a pendejo. Among friends it can be taken lightly, but for others it is better to be angry enough to back it up. Ironically, the Yiddish word for pendejo is a *putz* which means the same thing.

In high school I had a friend whose name I consistently forgot. I must have asked him for the umpteenth time when he finally yelled, "¡Olivas! !Pendejo!" So I called him Olivas Pendejo. At that same high school, we had a principal, Brother Alphonsus, whose favorite proverb was a reminder to students: *Naces pendejo, mueres pendejo!*— "You were born a pendejo, you will die a pendejo."

Proverbs on pendejos abound in Mexican culture: Children say what they are doing; old people recall what they

10

did; and pendejos say what they're going to do. Dogs open their eyes in fifteen days, pendejos never do. Of lovers that live far away from each other it is said, *Amor de lejos, amor de pendejos*—"Love from afar, love for pendejos." The word can also be used to relieve pain: *No hay pena que dure veinte años ni pendejo que la aguante*—"There is no pain that lasts twenty years nor a pendejo that will endure it."

El Diccionario de la Real Academia de la Lengua Española, (The Dictionary of the Royal Academy of the Spanish Language) defines pendejo as a "pubic hair." The secondary definition of a pendejo is a coward. Then there are tertiary definitions according to country: In Argentina, a pendejo is a boy who tries to act like an adult. In Colombia, El Salvador and Chile, a pendejo is a fool or a cocaine dealer. There are a lot of those in this country. Here and in Mexico a pendejo is more likely to be a fool or an idiot.

Señor Armando Jimenez, author of *Picardía Mexicana,* a collection of Mexican picaresque wit and wisdom, is also Mexico's foremost *pendejólogo* (pendejologist). According to Don Armando, the number of pendejos, even as you read this, is innumerable. It has been estimated that if pendejos could fly, the skies would be darkened and we would enter a new ice age. The pendejos would get a severe sunburn. Some pendejos go so far as to believe that if all pendejos were to be corraled, there would be no one left to close the corral gates. That theory has been discounted by the fact that herding pendejos would be like herding cats. Pendejos have a mind of their own.

The great majority of people regardless of class, color, or creed, are pendejos, according to Señor Jiménez. His research studies claim that up to 90% of the world population are pendejos. Of the remaining 10%, 5% are mentally unstable, .5% are geniuses, and 4% are unemployed—the exact amount needed for a sound economy. The remaining .5% are lost.

According to Jiménez, there are countless categories and types of pendejos. The following are but a few:

• The *políticos,* who think they will change the world with money, charisma or speeches.

• The hopeless pendejos, who blame all their problems on bad luck instead of the fact that they are pendejos.

• The happy ones, who believe in their superiority over other pendejos who look up to them.

• The dramatic pendejos, who can be identified at a distance of one city block, by their stance and by the way they walk, sometimes carrying a book or two.

• The pseudo-intellectuals, who act as if they are deep in thought on some theory when in reality they are wondering where they parked their cars.

• The optimistic pendejos, who are naive, happy, and talkative. They look for hidden treasures, mines, underground water. They also buy lottery tickets, bet on everything and believe in television wrestling.

• The pessimistic or doubting pendejos, who don't believe anything you tell them. If you don't believe this, you fall into this category. And if you do believe this, then you might fall into the category of those pendejos who believe everything.

• Entrepreneurial pendejos, who have grandiose projects, are eloquent, and make great salesmen. If this type convinces you, you are an even bigger pendejo.

This list may be used for self-evaluation, and to classify relatives, friends and lovers. If you did not find yourself in any of these pendejo groups, congratulations! This means you're either a genius, unemployed or mentally unstable. For those on the list, there is still no known cure, but you are not to blame. *Naces pendejo, mueres pendejo!*

C/S

The Joy of Jalapeños

In Mesoamerican cuisine, nothing compares with the gastronomic ecstasy that a hot jalapeño adds to the enjoyment of Mexican food. The piquant sensation on the tongue, the itch and tingling on the scalp, the beads of sweat on the forehead, the clearing of the sinus passages and the fogging of eyeglasses are all part of a cultural ritual in the ultimate Mexican eating experience.

Even among *Mexicanos,* many are invited but few are chosen to enjoy this seemingly masochistic practice of setting your mouth afire while nourishing your body and enjoying the food.

Like so many of my *paisanos,* I cannot, for the life of me, enjoy any type of food, whether it be gringo, Jewish or

Italian, without a good hot salsa, *jalapeños en escabeche, pico de gallo, chile de arbol, hecho al molcahete,* crushed red pepper, Tabasco sauce, Louisiana hot sauce, *chile habanero,* or just a fresh, dark green jalapeño.

Chile might have formed me into the kind of person I am, sometimes hot-tempered and passionate. Back home at the family table, we could always count on having two types of tortillas, *de maiz* or *harina,* beans and three types of chiles: *rojo, verde* and *fresco*—red, green and the fresh, unadulterated jalapeño in all of its luscious, dark green subtlety. Sometimes we had *hueros,* blonde yellow peppers, very innocent looking but just as deadly as the green ones. Other times we might have *serranos,* but while they were hot, they lacked the flavor of the jalapeño.

Father always went for the hottest one. If it was a dud, he would ask for another. Sometimes one chile was so hot that it took two meals to finish. Those gems were rare.

There is a whole process to evaluating a *salsa de chile,* and it's not by looking at the label to see if it was made in New Yawk City or Santone. First you study it in the bowl. If it's too tomatoey, it was probably made for tender tongues. With a spoon, you sift it to check its consistency, the spices used and how it was made: by roasting, cooking the peppers in water first, chopped in the blender or a Cuisinart. But the best flavor comes from the *molcahete.* After the chiles have been roasted and peeled, they are ground on a stone mortar. The stone flavor and the ground seeds add a special earthy taste.

A trained and experienced olfactory sense will tell you if it is hot or not. The fourth and final step in the examination is putting a small amount on the back of your hand and tasting it. Some like to use a corn chip but such interference dilutes the flavor. You need to know exactly how hot it is so you can add the correct amount to your food.

That ritual of tasting has all but disappeared with the sale of commercially made mild, medium, hot and very hot sauces. But there is nothing like homemade salsa. Contrary to popular belief, Mexican food is not hot, which is why salsas were created.

Tastes and preferences are personal, but I frown on restaurants that load the *salsa* with *cominos,* tomatoes and onions. The taste of those ingredients remain with you more than the jalapeño taste. Chiles, whether they be jalapeños or serranos, have their own peculiar tastes that should be enhanced, not hidden.

Nothing was more painful when I left home for the air force than to be served bland, gringo military food. That's where I developed a taste for common ordinary black pepper, Louisiana hot sauce or Tabasco. The S.O.S. eggs and sausage needed help. Since my departure from home I have forever yearned for salsas and fresh jalapeños.

From time to time when I was in the military, mother would send me care packages of canned *jalapeños en escabeche* or other forms of canned chile salsas. I was desperate and celebrated those few hot times, shedding tears of jalapeño joy with other Chicano buddies.

In Spain we introduced young Spanish women to what we told them were Mexican pickles. They had never heard of a jalapeño before. Their faces turned neon red.

In Zaragoza, Spain, a woman friend invited me to her home for dinner. Without jalapeños she made a sauce from crushed red pepper, spices and coñac. It was a fine moment in European gastronomic ingenuity.

My addiction for jalapeños is such that I confess to have eaten at exclusive restaurants and attended formal banquets with fresh jalapeños in my coat pocket. Banquet food can be boring and asking for the Tabasco sauce is a *faux pas.* If sitting with people who find such conduct reproachable, I simply cup my hands around the pepper and bite into it from time to time without their ever knowing. I have only been caught once, and another time a table companion confessed to me he wished he had brought jalapeños with him too.

Once I gave a humorous presentation at the annual California Rural Legal Assistance fundraising banquet. Before the presentation, while people were eating, I went around offering fresh jalapeños to go with their bland chicken. Some Hispanics were insulted and blushed while some Chicanos were delighted and blushed only after they bit into their dark green hot peppers.

To get the most out of a fresh jalapeño, especially one that has been refrigerated, it is necessary to get its hot juices flowing. Cup the pepper with both hands and blow warm breath onto it while rolling it between your palms. This is called "getting the jalapeño angry." It's supposed to get hotter if you curse it in Spanish.

Of course, there are many kinds of chiles but the jalapeño is king and named after the small town of Jalapa, Veracruz, where the character of the people is both piquant and picaresque. This is the same region that originated the dance and hot musical number "La Bamba," perhaps inspired by the effects of a jalapeño.

Much more can be said about this phallic plant food that can bring tears to the most macho of machos. With the Chicano movement, artists turned the jalapeño into

17

an icon, a symbol, an image representing the culinary, piquant and humorous aspect of Mexican culture. In a famous Mexican ballad, "La Llorona," the male singer cries out, *Yo soy como el chile verde, llorona, picoso pero sabroso*—"I am like the green chile, wailing woman, hot but delicious!"

The curative qualities and other little-known facts of the jalapeño and its pepper cousins are many.

Menudo, Mexican tripe soup, known as the national Mexican breakfast of champions, is known to cure hangovers. The truth: It is the chile in the menudo that activates the juices in your system and fights against alcohol dehydration.

According to Dr. T. F. Burks of the University of Arizona Health Sciences Center, hot peppers contain capsaicin, a chemical that is responsible for the piquancy and can effectively relieve certain types of pain. Like acupuncture, capsaicin blocks the nerve pathways that carry pain signals to the brain in chronic conditions such as pinched nerves and tumors.

A chile a day keeps the doctor away. U.S. Government studies show that people living in the Southwest have the lowest death rate from heart disease and cancer in the United States. One Doctor, Lora M. Shields, reported that chile may help rid the body of enough fats to lower cholesterol.

When the diet of the Otomi Indians of Central Mexico was studied by the Massachusetts Institute of Technology, their diet was found to be much more nutritious than the diet of a group of U.S. town dwellers. Since pre-Columbian times, the chile was used in folk medicine as a remedy for inflamed kidneys, chills, heart pains and tumors.

One ounce of chile contains as much as 20,000 units of vitamin A, which is twice the minimum daily requirement. Fresh chiles have even higher levels. One hundred grams of Texas green chile contains 235 mg. of vitamin C while a California orange has but 49 mg. Calcium content in chiles is also high.

According to *Albuquerque Living*'s Life Style poll in March 1987, Anglos prefer green chile and Latinos love red chile.

Curanderas, folk medicine healers, believe that hot chile peppers and salt on top of a cross made of nails can ward off witches.

In 1937 Dr. Albert Szent-Gyorgi was awarded the Nobel Prize in science for his studies of vitamin C in Paprika peppers, a cousin of the jalapeño.

Cold, insensitive feet or those with poor blood circulation have been revived by sprinkling socks or nylons with hot, red chile powder.

In 1982, Astronaut Bill Lenoir had an upset stomach that was linked to the jalapeño peppers he had carried into orbit. Eating and digesting chile is a process that takes some getting used to, especially in outer space. Start off slow and build up. Find a chile that you like, but that doesn't act like acupuncture, blocking your enjoyment of the food. But once you are *enchilado,* try to remain calm and not panic. People have gotten hurt when they run, trip, bump their heads or poison themselves by drinking the first liquid they see. Your best bet is dairy products: milk, sour cream, ice cream....

Dr. Paul Rozin of the University of Pennsylvania psychology department conducted a study of cultural food preferences, particularly for the chile pepper. According to

Dr. Rozin, chile aids digestion by stimulating gastric secretion and salivation, and helps to cool off the body by causing the face to sweat.

Furthermore, Dr. Rozin suspects that hot peppers trigger the release of endorphins, which are natural opiates of the brain, into the chili eater's system. So it may be that my addiction to jalapeños is caused not by cultural affiliation or heredity, but by endorphins.

C/s

The Great Taco War

In Redwood City, California, the Mexican flag was hoisted over the Taco Bell fast food restaurant and the local Mexican-American business community was angered and the flag was taken down. Taco Bell is determined to make inroads into the Mexican community through its culture and economics.

Tacos have become the hamburger's stiffest competitor as this country's favorite fast food. As of 1990, Taco Bell had already jumped ahead of McDonald's. But forget hamburgers for a couple of minutes. Today Taco Bell has not only infiltrated the *barrios* but has even opened its first restaurant in, of all places, Mexico City.

A Colonel Sander's Kentucky Fried Chicken restaurant in Beijing, or a McDonald's in Moscow does not seem as strange as a Taco Bell in the capital city of Mexico. I was already aghast at their having built a Taco Bell in San Francisco's Mission District, where Salsa music, bright murals, and traffic lights compete for attention, and where there is at least one *taquería* every two blocks.

In the Mission District, taquerías are San Francisco's nouvelle eating places. Yuppies and business executives from uptown dine elbow-to-elbow with *cholos* and other Latinos on exquisitely prepared designer-tacos and burritos made from charbroiled diced beef, chicken, pork, corned beef, tongue, brains, or veggies for vegetarians.

The taquerías are so popular that most customers are veritable connoisseurs of which is the talk o' the town. So it was brazen of Taco Bell to come into the Mission District and sell their mild imitations of the real thing. Even still they sold tacos to Chicanos and other Latinos in the barrio like they were going out of *estilo*.

¿Que paso? Taco Bell was competing with what some call the best taquerías north of the border. The news was so disturbing that the "Godfather of the Mission District," Rene Yañez, took me to see it. "You gotta write about this," he said.

This fast food restaurant came complete with California mission-style architecture and a yellow plastic bell. It was surrounded by a beauty salon, a Chinese restaurant, a hardware store, and a mattress store. In the morning, the Taco Bell corner serves as an unemployment line for Latinos in search of a day's work.

Taco Bell does brisk business. What seemed like a crowd from the outside was a slow, meandering line, Disneyland-style. This was better than walking into a burger place and wondering which line would move faster, only to get behind the guy ordering twenty Big Macs, ten regular fries, ten large fries, five diet cokes, five regular cokes, ten malts and two coffees for a hungry work crew.

The Taco Bell menu can be a mystery if one is not familiar with the renamed food items. They can even puzzle a bicultural person. What's an Enchirito? "A combination burrito and enchilada," the manager answered, half bored and following his response with a half-accusing glance at my ignorance. I had envisioned a half-burrito, half-enchilada transplant and felt the heartburn coming on.

They also featured Mexican pizza, which was a flat flour tortilla smothered with refried beans and topped with ground beef, cheese and shredded lettuce. But what were Cinammon Crispas? They were similar to *buñuelos,* fried flour tortillas generously sprinkled with sugar and cinammon.

Other items on the menu included the Nachos Bellgrande, Taco Bellgrande, and, of course, the kid's Fiesta Meal, which seemed incomplete without a piñata. They also listed steak Fajitas and chicken Fajitas, complete with the helpful phonetic spelling—"Fa-hee-tahs."

I ordered two tacos prepared with prefabricated hard tortilla shells at room temperature. Rene ordered the Mexican pizza. The meat was lukewarm and the cheese and shredded lettuce were cold. Halfway through the taco, the shell crumbled between my fingers and landed on my tray. Rene laughed and then I realized the reason for the plastic fork. When I finally got to taste my "taco" it was different and tasty in a funny sort of way. There is something surreal about having to tear a little plastic package with one's teeth in order to get to a salsa that is more mild and sweet than hot. Give me a dark green fresh jalapeño to sink my teeth into any day.

Orders are served in under five minutes and placed on a plastic tray with a paper placemat headlined, "The Border Run." It depicts an open highway in the desert leading to a Taco Bell and surrounded by highway signs that tell you to "Crack It, Bust It, Jump It, Snap it or Cross It" This, of course, is a subtle reference to crossing the border illegally or jumping a once-proposed fifteen-mile ditch south of San Diego. The hidden message is that eating at Taco Bell can be not only a treat but a real, live *Indiana Jones* adventure.

And who is the clientele in this Taco Bell in the barrio? *Los pobres,* poor people, seniors on fixed retirement incomes and immigrants who have "jumped, crossed or beat it" to this side. At 59 cents a taco, where else can a poor family eat for less than ten dollars with free drink refills? Where else can Latino teenagers hang out to socialize? Not at the barrio taquerías where tacos start at $1.50 each.

A typical day will find the outdoor seating of Taco Bell filled with Latinos of various ages. On one occasion a group of *batos locos,* crazy dudes, yelled at each other across the tables using foul *Español.* This didn't faze the older and younger women who kept right on conversing and eating. On a second visit, there was a whole day care nursery of some eighteen small fries, I mean, four and five-year-old children. Where else could they have afforded lunch?

In other parts of the city you can see the taco price war between Taco Bell and Jack-In-The-Box: 59 cents a taco,

49 cents a taco, 39 cents a taco, three for a dollar …
There's no end to the sales.

Not to be outdone, the Kentucky Fried Chicken in the
Mission District raised a banner selling: "Oven roasted
chicken with tortillas and salsa!" But finally the colonel
chickened out. The *pollo* fare was only on a trial basis.
Colonel Sanders may have been making a lot of *Yuan* in
downtown Beijing, but in the Mission District he was
losing *dinero* to tacos. The growing popularity of fast
Mexican food in barrios such as the Mission District will
be a significant turning point in the national taco war. Our
burritos and tacos are not only the real thing but our first
line of defense.

The fast food enterprise is cashing in on the unabashed
sale of Anglicized and commercialized Mexican food to
low-income Latinos, and the message is clear: "Hey! We
can't make it as good as you can, but we can sure sell it
faster and cheaper than you." Some hard-shelled Chicanos
and Mexicanos wouldn't be caught dead in one of these
Taco Bells. For others though, an empty stomach and
pocketbook do not distinguish the 'real' thing.

C/s

A Mixed Tex-Cal Marriage

According to Cecilia, my wife, we have a mixed marriage. She's from California, I'm from Texas. Though we have no regrets, this truly proves that love is blind.

When Cecilia and I first met, we thought we had a lot in common. As young, professional Chicanos in Washington, D.C., we both supported the United Farm Workers' grape and lettuce boycotts, the Coors boycott, the Gallo Wine boycott, the Farah Pants boycott, and the Frito Bandido boycott. We still boycott some of those items, for many reasons: health, habit, nostalgia or plain, ordinary guilt if we indulged in any of these.

As first generation Mexican-Americans, we both spoke

Español, graduated from Catholic schools and had similar politics.

But, as we were soon to discover, the vast desert that separates Texas and California also differentiates the culture and style of Chicanos. Because we met far from Texas and California, we had no idea at first at the severity of our differences.

We both liked enchiladas—the same enchiladas, I thought, until the first time Cecilia prepared them. They looked like enchiladas, and they smelled like enchiladas. And then I bit into one.

"These are good, *corazón*," I said. "But these are *entomatadas*. They have more tomato than chile. *Mí Mamá* used to make them all the time."

She threw me a piquant stare as I chewed away. "Hmmm, they're great!" I stressed through a mouthful.

Californians, like her parents who immigrated from the coastal state of Jalisco, Mexico, use more tomatoes than Texans like my parents, who came from the central states of Durango and Zacatecas and use more chiles.

Cecilia grew up with white *menudo*, tripe soup. White menudo? How could anyone eat colorless menudo? And not put hominy in it? Ours was red-hot and loaded with hominy. In Texas, we ate our menudo with bread. In California, it's with tortillas. Texas flour tortillas are thick and tasty, California flour tortillas are so thin you can see through them.

She didn't particularly like my Tony Lama boots or my country-western and Tex-Mex musical taste. I wasn't that crazy about Beach Boy music or her progressive, California-style country-western.

27

In California, the beach was relatively close for Cecilia. On our first date she asked how often I went to the beach from El Paso. Apparently, geography has never been a hot subject in California schools. That's understandable considering the sad state of education, especially geography, in this country. But in Texas, at one time the biggest state in the union, sizes and distances are most important.

In answer to Cecilia's question, I explained that to get to the closest beach from El Paso, I had to cross New Mexico, Arizona and California to reach San Diego. That's 791 freeway miles. The closest Texas beach is 841 freeway miles to the Gulf of Mexico.

Back when we were courting, California Chicanos saw *Texanos* as a little too *Mexicano,* still wet behind the ears, not assimilated enough, and speaking with either thick Spanish accents or "Taxes acksaints."

Generally speaking, Texanos saw their *Califas* counterparts as too weird, knowing too little if any Spanish and with speech that was too Anglicized.

After our marriage we settled in neutral Alexandria, Virginia, right across the Potomac from the nation's capital. We lived there a couple of years, and when our firstborn came, we decided to settle closer to home. But which home, Califas or Texas? In El Paso we wouldn't be close to the beach, but I thought there was an ocean of opportunity in that desert town. There was some Texas pride and machismo, to be sure. It was a tug-of-war that escalated to the point of seeking advice, and eventually I had to be realistic and agree that California had better opportunities. In EPT, the opportunities in my field were nonexistent.

The rest is relative bliss. Married since 1972, I'm totally

spoiled and laid-back in Northern Califas, but I still miss many of those things we took for granted in Texas, or Washington, D.C.—the seasonal changes, the snow, the heat, heating systems, autumn colors and monsoon rains; the smell of the desert after a rain, the silence and serenity of the desert, the magnified sounds of a fly or cricket, distant horizons uncluttered by trees, and the ability to find the four directions without any problem. I do miss the desert and, even more, the food. El Paso *is* the Mexican-food capital of this country.

Today, I like artichokes and appreciate a wide variety of vegetables and fruits. I even like white, colorless menudo and hardly ever drink beer. I drink wine, but it has to be a dry Chardonnay or Fume Blanc although a Pinot Noir or Cabernet Sauvignon goes great with meals. Although I still yearn for an ice cold Perla or Lone Star beer from Texas once in a while, Califas is my home now—mixed marriage and all.

C/s

Dear Mr. Consulate ...

Long before the Treaty of Guadalupe Hidalgo of 1847, when Northern Mexico became the Southwestern United States, *Mexicanos* have come and gone, sometimes with and sometimes without documentation. For centuries this migration was unimpeded until the Mexico/U.S. border was set up. Nevertheless, much natural "migration" continued relatively unhampered until the Great Depression, when *la migra,* the U.S. Immigration and Naturalization Service, began to clamp down. Since then, many Mexican citizens in this country have sought help by writing letters to the Mexican Consulate offices throughout the United States. These exiles were honest, hard-working Mexican farm workers with little or no formal schooling who needed help with all kinds of problems.

Some time ago, an *amigo Texano* gave me a photocopied collection of some of these letters written to Mexican consulate offices throughout the United States from the thirties to the early sixties. The unpublished collection is from the Rómulo Munguia Collection, the Mexican-American Archives, in the Latin American Collection in Austin, Texas.

The following samples from those letters are presented here with all due respect, for many of these are men and women, who, to this day continue to struggle and labor in this country against incredible odds. Some of these letters were written in phonetic Spanish. It is likely that some were written by those who professed to know the art of letter writing. Some are humorous, some are painful. The following are some of the addresses on the envelopes:

- Mexican Headquarters
- Mexican Konsulate General
  West Houstin St., Alamo, Tex., U.S.
- Casualty of Mexico
- Mr. Console of Mexico
  Custom Bldg.
- Consolation General of Mexico
- Consoled General Mexicano
- Official Consular Mail Free
- Consulado General
  Bexar County Jail Mexico
- Mexican Pass-port Office

- To the Sr. Consulado General de México
  who is in Nogales, Arizona
- Sr. Consul Mexican
  Ostin, Texas (Austin)
- Menfis, Tenesí
  Please deliver to the Consulate General
  Mexicano in *Los Estados Unidos*
- Mister Tucson, Arizona
- Consul Manager of the Republic of Mexico

The return address for one letter was "For Wes," Texas. Another spelled it "Forowes." One person addressed his or her letter to the Department of Protection of the Mexican Consulate.

The body of the letters includes one man who complained, "... I don't own a radio or receive the newspaper so I wasn't aware that all Mexicanos had to leave their *huellas vegetales*"—vegetables prints, instead of digital prints.

One man wanted a guarantee that he would be able to return to Mexico with a "Senith" radio he had bought. He signed, "with confidence, inexorable courtesies and hopes for an answer in the affirmative."

A man named Músquiz wrote, "In view of the fact that I now find myself in this Hotel Laredo County Jail and that I had vacation time coming and now will have to pass them here, I request you do me the favor of interceding. Please do not have me fall in the hands of immigration, you have me here at your service and disposition."

One mail-order herb salesman complained to the Mexican consul general, "I believe you should have defended me since they took my post office box away because I received money for herbs that I sold; but I see that you have slow blood circulating through your veins because you did not get 'hot enough' to defend me. You should understand that all human beings have the right of struggle for life. I sell herbs to make a living. If someone asks me for an herb for the stomach, I send them what I think will help them. And if it doesn't help them, it is not my fault but theirs for having believed me. This is business, pure and legitimate." "*Sí, señor,*" he continued, "God gave us the right to fight in a struggle. Can't you see that our father, Adam, when he was about to expire, called to his deathbed his one hundred children and told them, 'My children, I leave you; make a living from the stupid.' And so, I struggle through a divine mandate, so why do you let the law take away my post office box? Answer me, let's see, answer me." Signed, "Your crushed co-patriot, Ramirez, Tilden, Texas, 1931."

A Señor Morales addressed the Mexican Consulate, "Dear Sir, Defender of Mexicanos, Since there is no more work in Texas, for Mexicanos, I have decided to repatriate myself to Mexico, but before hitting the road, I would like you to let me know if I will have to pay taxes for those things which I am returning with. I don't think you should charge me because I can swear before a notary public that all that I have with me is second-hand. And here goes the list of what I want to take with me: My wife, Juana Farías; my daugher Mariana; my daughter Chona; my son, Masidonio ... plates, cups, knives, forks; three red women's panties, four green women's panties; a night basinet, one water syringe, one old Chevy pickup truck ..."

On 29 June 1945, a Señor Peña wrote the Arts and Sciences Department of the Mexican Consulate: "I expose you to a wise secret which I have discovered of how to make the mute talk again. I would place myself before you in an examination with four of five people who bring their children with that natural condition, fathers, mothers or tutors, and they will all leave very happy because from that day on they will be able to communicate with others through the medium of their voice."

One succint letter cried out, "Most appreciated sir, the present in which I have the honor of presiding is with the objective of asking for your help to get me out of this prison," signed, "Your attentive prisoner."

One poor man in a mental institution wrote to the "Onoravle Koncul Jeneral Mexicano" in San Antonio, Texas: "Sometime ago I was looking for Pancho Villa in the Revolution, Gesus Cristo in the insomnia COC, hospice of human infirmities of the mind and Guadalupe Gutierrez of the #8 precinct, of the Candelarias or Candelarias Road, County of Vernalillo, City of Albuquerque, New Mexico. I, his brother Iscariot, in the insomnia C41 of the Revolution, Maximilian of the same Austria I Max Gutierrez . . ."

A budding entrepreneur wrote, "I am a working man who would like to get into the egg business in Mexico. I talked to a certain man who before getting arrested for being a little too happy told me that you have much experience in these matters and that you could help me . . . I can sell my eggs at a cheap price because I have chickens and they lay big eggs, although they are not very white, but their quality is the same according to my health permit. Answer me soon so that I may know how to transport my eggs, since I don't want them to get old while I sit around here unemployed. There is no market for them here."

"Honorable Sir:" wrote one father, "With all due respect I direct myself to you pleading to know in the most attentive manner on the matter of the death of my son Rosendo who contracted work as a *bracero* . . . Without knowing to this date, the cause that originated the death of my son or motive that might have originated the death."

One letter sounds more ancient than its 1954 date: "Most Illustrious and Unique Sir: Considering that longevity and perseverance are doted with double virtue, I await your honorable designees who will dignify to alleviate this difficulty and that you may be the sufficient and valid defender of my brother, who finds himself a prisoner in La Tuna, Texas, according to a communication dated the 13th of the present from that institution.

"And you, whose investiture is loved by the wise, celebrated by the great and from whom I expect a testimonial of thy invective favor of interpolation, informing me as I beg of you dearly the state that my brother keeps in his detention and I embrace the hope that thy favor will defend him and set him free, that perhaps due to ignorance he crossed illegally into his precarious situation. Respectfully . . ." The man signed his name, and added his thumbprint.

C/s

All the Things
I Learned in School Weren't
Necessarily True

Perhaps the most memorable experiences one has in school are those that come into direct conflict with one's family's beliefs and traditions. Almost everyone goes through these challenging and unforgettable moments.

My earliest conflict came in kindergarten, when I was given a quiz about nature. "Can the sun shine while it is raining at the same time?" Of course! I had seen it. So I checked off "Yes." In El Paso it happened all the time, and forty some years later it still happens. Throughout the Southwest it is a very natural occurrence for many though a phenomenon for others. For Sister Margaret Ann, it was a phenomenon because she had never paid attention.

According to Sister, I was wrong so she put a big, fat,

red "X" by my "yes" box. I found it impossible to defend my answer because of the ridicule I received and the anger I felt. In El Paso I can be wincing at the sun and getting wet at the same time. I can drive in and out of flash floods as easy as going from one block to the next.

Four years later, Sister Mary Justin, my fourth-grade teacher told us that God could not do everything. "He can only do what is possible," said Sister Justin. "For instance, God cannot make a circle a square or vice versa or make one plus one equal one."

Well, I didn't believe that for one instant. God could do everything and anything that was good. To change a circle into a square or vice versa was totally plausible. It was a challenge and I eventually solved the impossible divine task so that even a human could change a circle to a square. By making the square out of a piece of string, I could easily transform it into a circle, or could make a squared circle or a circled square. Since then I have also learned that one plus one is not necessarily two and that God is a she and also goes by the name *Quetzalcoatl*.

Then there was Mrs. Roth, our music teacher, who expected all of the sixth-grade class to open their mouths wide to sing and enunciate each syllable to the fullest. The majority of the class was Mexican-American so she decided to tell us that the lines on old Mexican faces were due to the fact that these people didn't open their mouths and enunciate properly when they talked. As sixth graders we weren't ready to hear about age lines on our faces, never mind the fact that we knew those lines were due to old age or a merciless desert sun that engraves character into a face.

Since my school days, many beliefs have gone down the

tube. I can still remember books with black-and-white photos or color illustrations of what used to be considered a healthy diet: eggs, whole milk, cheese and meat. Today, we get a whole different message: "Fat City," with a capital C for cholesterol.

My Roman Catholic religion has also gone through tremendous reformations. Back then, if anything was questioned it was tantamount to sacrilege. Faith, hope and charity were the magic words.

In retrospect, some beliefs were outrageously funny, if not strange. Whatever happened to "ejaculations?" Spiritual ejaculations were short profound prayerful utterings. Each time one was recited the person got so many days of indulgence (another one of those funny words). A favorite was 360 days off from purgatory each time someone uttered a spiritual ejaculation. I ejaculated so many times that I must have at least twenty years credit towards time off from purgatory.

Unfortunately, Pope John Paul closed down purgatory when he came to power. Was it closed down because the same overcrowding problem we have in our jails and penitentiaries here on earth? Was it a budget problem? Was everybody in purgatory pardoned and sent up to heaven? Were some sent to the eternal fires of hell? What kind of credit can I get for my ejaculations now? These questions remain unanswered.

Limbo was also closed down. All those unbaptized babies didn't qualify for heaven, so they were put in limbo. Like these babies, Chicanos have always been in limbo—neither here nor there.

Latin mass was dropped, along with saints such as St.

Patrick and St. Christopher. I graduated from St. Patrick's Grade School and devoutly attended hundreds of masses at St. Patrick's church. Now St. Pat's is nothing but a myth, and St. Christopher was dropped from thousands of automobile dashboards and key chains. Yet St. Christopher continues as the patron saint of the undocumented and the coyotes who help them cross the Río Grande. Somebody must have thought him up from Christopher Columbus, the first wetback to survive crossing a deep divide and wet the dry American soil.

Eating meat on Fridays was a God-fearing sin. Comedian George Carlin had a whole number about that, as he wondered whatever happened to those people doing time on a meat rap. But I didn't have to sin to eat meat on Fridays. On this day I would cross the international border into Ciudad Juarez, Mexico, where it was not a sin, and I could gorge on all the meat tacos I wanted without fear of the eternal fires of hell. There were even times on the U.S. side when we had a countdown to midnight, Friday, to dig into a meat sandwich, a taco or a hamburger already in our grubby hands.

Pagan babies were also popular in my Catholic school days. Any kid could adopt one, name it and give money for it through the missions. These were Third-World babies that were supposed to be starving for God and bread. Their brown skin and beautiful big brown eyes were supposed to say it all.

Certain movies were forbidden to Catholics by the Catholic League of Decency under penalty of automatic excommunication. *Blue Moon* was one of the first movies to be considered immoral and depraved. Does anyone remember that movie?

That must have been the first shovelful of dirt to reach the depths of depravity with *Deep Throat,* a real choker.

In those days, to be gay was to be happy and joyous, masturbation could cause blindness and family planning was sinful.

We learned a lot back then. Some of what we learned were fallacies, some were not, and some only reflected different morals and values. But we survived, and can now look back and laugh.

But no learning experience was more painful or damaging than the silence imposed on our Mexican culture, history and beautiful Spanish language. To speak Spanish was not only illegal but also a sin: "Bless me Father, for I have sinned. I spoke Spanish in class and during recess. . . ." *Mea culpa, mea culpa, mea máxima culpa!* I gently rapped my closed fist on my chest. I knew I would sin again but that was all right because there was always confession, now called "reconciliation."

The silence of our language, culture, and history was broken at home by our Mother, a former school teacher in Mexico. She taught her six children to know, love and respect our language, our customs and our history.

And this is one reason why I write—to express those beliefs and to teach what was once a silent sin. These words etched in black ink are made not from individual letters but scars that perforate the paper-like open wounds to the soul of a young Chicano who sought the truth in his own reflection.

Blessed be the teachings of many cultures in the class-rooms! Blessed be the truth in her many fashions and forms! Blessed be God in her glory and wisdom!

C/s

La Cuetlaxochitl

The popular Chistmas flower known as the Poinsettia in this country was first called a *cuetlaxochitl* (coo-eht-la-soch-itl) by the Aztecs. It represented purity, and its name signified: "Flower that withers, mortal flower that perishes like all that is pure." The cuetlaxochitl was cultivated as an exotic gift from nature and admired but never touched. Its bright red color had been given by some god as a reminder of the periodic sacrificial offerings in accordance with the creation of the Fifth Sun.

The intense red color represented *chalchilmatl*, the precious liquid, the blood of the sacrifices offered to the gods.

Beautiful botanical gardens existed throughout the Aztec empire in pre-Hispanic times. Flowers and herbal plants were cultivated for their beauty and medicinal purposes. From October to mid-May, the cuetlaxochitl was admired and observed as it flowered like "birds aflame." Circa 1440–1446, the great Aztec leader Tlacaélel and his half-brother Moctezuma Ilhuicamina visited the most beautiful of these gardens in Oaxatepec, in what is now the Mexican state of Morelos, and revitalized the cuetlaxochitl there as reminders of blood sacrifices.

One legend explains their origin from sixteenth-century Mexico. Franciscan friars evangelizing the area of Taxco celebrated one Chistmas with a lavishly decorated nativity scene. Once, when a miracle occured that frightened off many of the faithful, the rosary and a litany were prayed, a piñata was broken, gifts were exchanged, and a mass was held. The flowers turned red. After that night, the flower was named *flor de nochebuena,* Flower of the Blessed Night.

Many other legends sprang forth, including one about a young child who had nothing to offer the Baby Jesus but a handful of weeds. When she presented them at the nativity scene, the weeds turned into beautiful, red flowers.

During the following centuries the flor de nochebuena, or cuetlaxochitl, became a symbol of Christmas and Mexico's evangelization. In earlier times, the flower's bloom in October signaled the coming of Christmas.

The flower spread thoughout the Mexican states. In Chiapas it is known as *Sijoyó,* in Durango as Catalina, in Guerrero, Michoacán, Veracruz and Hidalgo it is known as *Flor de Pascua,* and in Oaxaca as *Flor de Santa Catarina.*

Chile and Peru call it the "Crown of the Andes," and in Argentina it became the Federal Star because it served as a symbol for the republicans in their liberation struggle. Today it is their *flor nacional.*

In this country, the flower has another history and another name but its origin is still Mexican. It all began when Joel Robert Poinsett was appointed as ambassador to Mexico. On Christmas day 1825, Ambassador Poinsett visited the Taxco church of Santa Prisca, where the Franciscans had adorned the nativity scene with strange big flowers that gave it a very elegant and uncommon appearance.

Enamored by the flower named Nochebuena, he shipped some to his friends back home in Charleston, South Carolina. This was the origin of naming these flowers Poinsettias in this country.

Ambassador Joel Poinsett was a multitalented man. He studied medicine in England and was an amateur architect who built a state road, a bridge with a Gothic arch and a church in South Carolina. He was a congressman and an unofficial U.S. ambassador to South America and Europe. Early in Poinsett's carreer, prior to his Mexican ambassadorship, President Martin Van Buren, who served between 1836 and 1840, apppointed him Secretary of War. Besides being a botanist who traded seeds with friends on a worldwide basis, Poinsett was also an unabashed nationalist, experimenting with war rockets, lobbying for a national powder factory, and without success tried to establish a military draft system. He increased the size of the army by a third and many of his soldiers, helped transport Indians westward. During Poinsett's term as secretary of war, more Indians were displaced than at any other time.

While ambassador, Poinsett meddled so much in the affairs of Mexico and the rest of Latin America that the term *Poinsettismo* was coined to describe officious and intrusive conduct. Poinsett was finally declared *persona non grata* by the exasperated Mexican government when he took sides in a political dispute. With his life in danger, Poinsett was recalled to Washington on Chistmas day, 1829.

During the last years of his life, Poinsett continued to cultivate the flower throughout the South as a symbol of Christmas and succeeded in making a small fortune by introducing it to the United States and the rest of the world.

It is ironic that the flower that originally symbolized Aztec blood sacrifices, also came to symbolize the blood of Christ, Christmas and the blood sacrifices of a U.S. Secretary of War who drove more Indians from their homes than any other government official.

Poinsett helped found the National Institute for the Promotion of Science and Useful Arts, a precursor of the Smithsonian Institute. According to Dr. Robert Faden, a botanist at the Smithsonian Institute's National Museum of Natural History, the poinsettia belongs to a large and fascinating species of plants, the Euphobiaceae, that might provide a cleaner, renewable substitute for gasoline and other fossil fuels.

Five hundred years after the encounter between Europe and this continent, we should attempt to recapture the history and contributions of the indigenous peoples. It would be a noble act to give the flower its original name, cuetlaxochitl—"Flower that whithers, flower that perishes like all that is pure"—as a reminder of wounded Mother Earth.

C/s

44

Return to the Mother Land

Ciudad de México. I continue to be struck by the contrasts within Mexico and between that country and the United States. Though I was born and raised on the border, these contrasts seem to me more and more severe each year.

On the sidewalks of the wide *avenidas,* on the narrow side streets and in the Metro subway of the biggest city on earth, 500 years after the conquest, I can still distinguish the Criollos from the Indios and the Mestizos. Not many Mexicanos make that distinction any more. Many white Euro-Mexicanos will shrug their shoulders, declare they are 100 percent Mexican. Unlike the people in this country, Mexicanos do not partition or categorize their ancestry. On the contrary, offense is taken if they are questioned about their background.

In Spanish-colonial Mexico, Criollos (Mexicanos of pure Spanish parentage) were looked down upon by the mainland Spaniards. The experience of the Criollos paralleled that of the Chicanos. Born in the United States but of Mexican parentage, Chicanos don't necessarily qualify for first-class citizenship or acceptance. But this comparison is short-lived because Chicanos recognize the racial and cultural complexity of their makeup: Chicanos recognize they are Indios, Hispanos, Mexicanos and United States citizens. José Vasconcelos' theory of *La Raza Cosmica* has more validity in this country with the Chicano than with the Mexicano.

Mexicanos will tell you they are all one—"*¡Puros Mexicanos!*" But as in the United States, not all are equal in the eyes of justice, education and economic opportunity.

¡En México no hay racismo! Too many Mexicanos will tell you and insist it is classism. *¡Es la clase y la pobreza!* Yes, you become more class conscious in Mexico, but race also matters. Who drives the taxi cabs? Who sells newspapers? Who dresses well? Who is in military uniform?

Indeed, who is in military uniform? Every September 16, Mexico's day of independence, a military parade marches through the Zócalo, in front of the *presidente* and down *El Paseo de la Reforma*. This formidable parade features not only the latest tanks and troop carriers, but also hundreds of young *soldados Méxicanos, cien porciento Indios,* proud and immaculate in their military outfits. Their physiognomy is no different than the troops Moctezuma commanded 500 years ago.

46

Moctezuma's troops in modern army uniforms, an irony, the conquered and the oppressed becoming the first line of defense. And it is no different in the United States, where the ancestors of slaves and "wetbacks" make up the backbone of the military. No matter what Hollywood movies say, African-Americans and Chicanos have taken the brunt of the war casualties since World War II.

The biggest city in the world is choking with its own smog and poor people. (And these poor people don't even contribute to the smog.) But the fashionably dressed professionals drive or are driven around with an aura of importance—left-over Criollos and Mestizos with a few Indian faces sprinkled among the elite.

At the Metro subway ticket window an indigenous family of five has a conference. They look as lost as *turistas* on their first day in the city. But theirs is a different preoccupation as they slowly count pesos among themselves to see if they can afford the fare. My heart goes out to them and I want to give them something but maybe they do have enough and I don't want to be condescending. But I am Mexicano too, and I am human. I vacillate and sometimes give, depending on situation and intuition. Mestizos and Indios from the *provincias* and *campesinos* from the *campo* continue to flock into the biggest city in the world. The Indio has come down from the mountain.

Mexico, land that my parents left so long long ago. Their memory lingers in Agustín Lara songs—*Farolito, Solamente Una Vez, Noche de Ronda*—and in the familiar sounds of the Spanish language.

I overhear familiar conversations. I'm home, I'm not a stranger though I was not born in Mexico. But I'm no

longer Mexicano ... I think ... I pause with indecision. I
don't know. Mexico has grabbed me back—*México lindo y
querido*—"My beautiful and beloved Mexico"; but so has
my good ole U.S. of A.

On a radio interview I am asked, "Pardon the question,
but do you write as a Mexicano, or ... what?" Eager for the
question that I have anticipated for years, I answer, "I
write as a Mexicano and I write as a gringo. I am a
Mexicano and I am a gringo!" I say it with pride and
conviction, for what else is a Chicano?

Each time I return to Mexico I find the term Chicano
more and more acceptable. The word finally begins to sink
in as it struggles to survive in the States against the term
Hispanic.

It shows the speed of change in a country steeped in
tradition. For Mexico, Chicano is a better choice than
Hispanic. For Mexicanos, it makes more sense than "Hispanic," a term too generic and European for a people that
are more indigenous in appearance and culture.

The late great Mexican artist Rufino Tamayo was asked
in an interview by the Chicano art historian, Ramón Favela, why he did not like the term "Chicano." Tamayo
refused to answer though Favela kept asking. Finally,
Tamayo cringed and exploded, "Because I just don't like
it!" For many Mexicanos, the word Chicano is still like the
screech of chalk on a blackboard. It makes their skin
quiver down to their toe nails.

"What's in a word?" asks one Mexico City columnist
when writing about the word Chicano. If Chicano was a
pejorative term at one time, so was the term *Judío,* Jewish. During the Spanish Inqusition, Jews were called *mar-
ranos,* pigs.

My wife, Cecilia, and I gave a series of talks in Mexico City on Chicano culture, higher education and feminism. For several days we fielded questions from inquisitive and interested Mexicanos. Always they begin with the most basic, "What is a Chicano?" We answer, and they come back, "*Sí*, but what does it mean?" With time, definitions change and answers become longer and more complex.

A Chicano is both Hispanic and Indian. The term "Hispanic" alone negates our Indian heritage. Our ancestors were not only the conquistadores but also the conquered. It is our vanquished heritage that has always haunted us and been ignored.

Chicano is more than a political label for it has a link to our indigenous past. Its etymology dates to the conquest of the *Valle de Mexica*. Mexica was pronounced "Meshica." The Spaniards had no letter or sound in their alphabet for the *Nahuatl* "sh" or hard "j" so they put an "x" in its place. Meshico became México and Tejas, Texas. The first Mestizos were born of Spanish soldiers and indigenous maidens. This scorned underclass of "half-breeds" were called *meshicanos*, which evolved to *shicanos*. Chicanos is nothing more than an abbreviated form for Mexicanos.

Until recently, the term Chicano was so abhorred in Mexico that much of the media preferred to use Mexicano-Americano. In "Labyrinth of Solitude," Octavio Paz, Mexico's Nobel poet and philosopher, avoided the term "Chicano" though it was already a common term. However, he did write of the *Pachuco*, the Chicano zoot-suiter of the '40s. Years later and after the Chicano movement this essay has returned to haunt him as superficial and erroneous.

In another essay on the Mexican character, Paz wrote of

the "Hispanic thesis which would have us descend from Cortés to the exclusion of La Malinche," the Indian interpreter and mistress to Cortés and mother of two of his children.

Paz stated, "The Mexican does not want to be either an Indian or a Spaniard. Nor does he want to be descended from them. And he does not affirm himself as a mixture, but rather as an abstraction." A Chicano in this country confronts reality and identifies as both, claims his full ancestry, and affirms himself as a mixture, a true "mexture." Hispanic is half the truth, half a lie.

At the beginning of this century, Mexicans called any Mexicano who crossed the border and lost his Mexican culture a Chicano—a traitor. Many of those immigrants were poor, rural Mestizos shunned by both countries.

We inherited traits from our Indian ancestors. Mexican cuisine is Mesoamerican, not Mediterranean. Mexican music has Moorish and indigenous influences. The colors on a *razartista's* palette are not the muted pastels reflecting the cold, gray, eastern skies but brilliant earth colors under a burning sunlit desert sky. The drama and passion of our culture is reflected in our desert sunrises and sunsets.

Andrés Segura, a Mexico City Aztec dance general and teacher of Aztec thought and culture, views the Chicano as the ultimate extension of the Mesoamerican Indian. According to Aztec prophecy, their descendants would return to Aztlán, to the Southwest.

To be a Chicano in the political sense is to know history and our ancestral investment in blood, sweat and tears. The 1970 East Los Angeles Moratorium, the walkouts, boycotts and protest marches were not led by Hispanics but by Chicanos. Twenty years ago while Woodstock partied, Blacks, Indios and Chicanos battled for civil rights.

The generic term Hispanic attempts to unite a whole country of diverse Latinos from Afro-Hispanics to Anglo-Hispanics. As a handle it has been convenient for the government, the media and the corporate world.

However, mere labels don't make a difference in education, median incomes and political representation. Numbers are power, but the seams and splits still show. Cuban-Americans and Mexican-Americans occupy opposite ends of the political spectrum. The melting pot theory has proven a myth for Hispanics.

Who is a Chicano? Anyone born of Mexican ancestry in the United States. It includes those whose ancestors go back to the Indio-Hispanic roots of the Southwest. It can also include those born in Mexico or other Latin American countries but raised in the United States who identify with Chicanos. It has been a term of choice for many. Today some young people shy away from the term Chicano in favor of the more acceptable mainstream Hispanic, or Mexican-American.

During my military service from 1960 to 1964, the term "Chicano" was popular among many of us Mexican-Americans from the Southwest. We socialized and communicated using a combination of English, Spanish and the Chicano dialect of Caló. We proudly called ourselves Chicanos back then.

It was hard for many Mexican parents to accept the word "Chicano" when the movement came. They were puzzled and pained because they knew how pejorative the term was. They may have even used it pejoratively and now they had children that called themselves Chicanos.

51

My parents' first acceptance was to nickname our brown 1964 Plymouth Valiant, *el Chicanito*. It was cute, not to be taken seriously. For Mexicanos from Mexico we were plain and simple *pochos,* spoiled fruit, the literal translation of the word. We had lost our *sabor,* our *Mexicanidad.*

Times change and time changes. We are now invited to Mexico as Chicanos, to speak as Chicanos, as *poetas,* as *artistas.* While many turn Hispanic, some of us continue as Chicanos because we remember the price. Too much blood had been shed to simply check off Hispanic when we fill out the form. The term is but another way to oppress us and negate our history. Consciously or unconsciously the term is used stop the evolution of Chicanos.

Another popular question in our Mexico City talks? Why is the Mexican revolutionary Emiliano Zapata a Chicano hero? What does he have to do with Chicanos? Pancho Villa would make more sense since he was from the northern state of Chihuahua. Zapata was from the South and came to this country as a hero and important symbol to campesinos, for the United Farm Workers. When they immigrated from Mexico they brought Emiliano Zapata and the Virgin of Guadalupe, two strong symbols of the United Farm Workers.

Some Mexicanos remain puzzled. "But you Chicanos don't understand. Emiliano Zapata and Pancho Villa were common criminals and thieves," they insist. Perhaps, but they championed the cause of the poor and oppressed. Besides being revolutionaries, they were avengers. Chicanos have such heroes of their own including Joaquín Murrieta, Tiburcio Vásquez and Gregorio Cortez. In Anglo-American folklore and history, they were colorful outlaws from the lawless west. But for Chicanos, they were nothing less than avengers resisting the Yankee invasion.

On a Wednesday morning, we met with some thirty *Chicanologos* at the Autonomous Mexican University of Xochimilco. Professors and investigators from various universities around Mexico City met to present their studies of Chicanos and the Mexican migration North. The majority were anthropologists studying the migration habits of their countrymen to *el Norte* and their return. Fascinating projects and findings came to light. Many of these Chicanologists began their study by migrating north as undocumented workers and doing their work in the fields working alongside their *paisanos*. There are whole Mexican *pueblos* which serve as direct but unofficial conduits and labor sources to specific communities in the Southwest, such as between Aguililla, Michoacán and Redwood City, California.

Mexico is now acutely concerned about the flight of youth, talent and labor force to el Norte. It is no longer just the lower-income class but the middle class that is crossing the border. This is likely to make Mexico more democratic and capitalist; and the United States more sensitive—hopefully.

One investigator pointed out that migrant women got a taste of equality while working in the United States, and when they returned to Mexico took up their secondary role with much frustration. That too is changing in Mexico.

In reference to the stereotype of what a Chicano is in Mexico, I reminded them that Chicanos are children of exiles, children of revolutionaries, children of undocumented workers, children abandoned by the Mother Country, children of parents who sought work, sought bread, children they did not educate. They were hard words but I softened them with the reminder that we were prodigal children returning.

What still separates Chicanos from Mexicanos? The language barrier and resentment. While many Chicanos may be bilingual, many are limited in their Spanish especially when discussing complex subjects. A Chicano in Mexico can feel very out of place because he may look indian but talk like a gringo. Educated and professional Chicanos can appear mute and dumb in their mother country if they have not mastered Spanish.

I have seen many Anglo-Americans have an easier time mastering Spanish language, but with Chicanos, there seems to be a barrier, a phobia that is more psychological than people realize. There is a resentment for past treatment. We have scars, and they appear when we talk our mother tongue.

At one question and answer period we were corrected for our use of Mexico-Americano, instead of *Mexicano-Norteamericano.* Cecilia quickly replied that it was exactly that type of correction and trivial criticism that kept us apart and prevented Chicanos from communicating, relating, and learning.

The conferences came to a poignant end on a Friday night when my book, *Weedee Peepo,* was presented in a symposium in Coyoacán. Three Mexican writers who had become good friends on other trips spoke favorably of the book but also criticized the Spanish translations by a combination of editors.

After their comments, the microphone on the table was passed to me. I could not talk. My throat and my eyes were about to betray me. I sat there, stone-faced, not uttering a word. Twice I began to speak, and twice my throat failed me. The third time I swallowed the knot and spoke ... about my Mexican parents. Had they only lived to see my return to *la capital* of the country they loved so much but had to leave. I spoke of my mother's ancestors, who go back to José Antonio Torres, *El Amo,* one of the heroes of the Mexican War of Independence against Spain.

Today, Cecilia and I are first-generation Mexican-Americans, parents of second-generation Mexican-Americans. Since the death of my parents, our ties with relatives in Mexico have slowly dissipated. But this too is part of the Chicano revolution, an independence from those feelings of shame, hate and guilt that we may have experienced because of Mexico. I can still clearly and proudly see my ancestry going back to the Mexican War of Independence. But we are now from this side of the border and part of a new era of awareness and independence. Mexico is closer to the Southwest now than when it was theirs. Mexico never left the Southwest, it just learned English.

C/S

Passive Resistance

Tepetlixpa, Mexico. September, 1986. We drove from the biggest city in the world to this ancient Aztec *pueblo*. Nahuatl is still spoken here and many ancient traditions continue. Tepetlixpa is two hours from Mexico City, beneath the ageless Popocatepetl, a dormant volcano wrapped in a romantic myth about an Aztec warrior returning from battle to find his love Ixtlacihuatl, a companion volcano, in an eternal sleep.

Five hours earlier, in a Mexico City hotel, I had called Andrés Segura, an old friend. I was in Mexico to do research on *maíz*, corn, for a mural. Immediately he scolded me and insisted I go with him to a *velada*, an all-night vigil in Tepetlixpa. "You don't consult books and murals to

56

learn about maíz. Come listen to the pueblo that knows it and grows it."

At 8:30 that night a taxi drives me to Andrés' home. Four other members of his Aztec dance troupe arrive, including Emilio, Andrés' brother, who sits in a wheelchair because of deformative arthritis. Andrés, 55, is a healer and spiritual leader who has been able to alleviate Emilio's pain.

Andrés is also a general of the Aztec dance. Well known in Mexico, he travelled and lived throughout the Southwest during the late sixties and seventies, teaching Aztec thought and culture. His first language is Nahuatl, but he speaks Spanish, some English, and a smattering of other European languages he has picked up on his travels.

In Tepetlixpa we will pray for rain. The *milpas,* corn fields, are in full bloom and need rain.

As we drive to Tepetlixpa, Andrés and I monopolize the conversation talking about old mutual friends and the Chicano movement. It's been years since he has been to the States. To illustrate what is happening in the United States, I refer to a mural in Mérida, Yucatán. It depicts a battle scene between Mayan Indians and Spanish soldiers. Underneath is a plaque with the words, ". . . they conquered us, but our culture conquered them." That is what is happening in *los Estados Unidos,* I tell him. The music, language, architecture, dance, food and dress is strongly being influenced by Indio-Hispanics.

Andrés does not like my reference to the conquest. "We have not been conquered. We have been invaded but we have not been conquered. What we have is passive resistance." Andrés is still an Aztec in thought, word and culture. "This is passive resistance, much of it unconscious," he says.

Andrés asks about various Chicano friends and the projects they are involved in. Like a concerned godfather, he questions some projects, comments on others but overall, he approves and is satisfied.

We arrive in Tepetlixpa too soon and the conversation ends. It is midnight as we drive slowly through the dusty, potholed streets that look and feel more like *arroyos secos,* dry streams. The car stops in front of an old, wooden portal door with a naked bulb hanging above it. The portal doors open, and we are met by a singing crowd of women, men, children and elders. They hold religious banners of the *Virgen de Guadalupe* and of *Jesucristo.* Andrés and his troupe join the hymns even while they are still in the car. The chants are in Spanish but accentuated with the beat of Aztec drums and *charangas,* mandolins made from armadillos.

Everyone greets everyone as we enter a dirt floor adobe room, approximately fifteen by thirty feet. At the front end of the room is a makeshift altar covering the entire wall, filled with carnations and other white flowers, along with candles, statues of saints and a crucifix. In front of the altar is a square blue tablecloth with four votive candles on each end and one in the middle, the four directions and the center. There are benches made from wooden planks resting on empty Pepsi Cola and Coca Cola cases. This is passive resistance.

The singing continues long after everyone has entered and taken their seats. The hymn finally comes to an end and formal welcomes are given by the elders. Andrés thanks them for having been invited to lead the *velada.*

He then introduces me as a brother from *el Norte* who is with them in spirit and struggle. I feel at home with them and express my gratitude but am at a loss for words to say how much more I feel.

The hymns continue in Spanish, but the arrangement and the rhythm is indigenous. Two women begin a floral arrangement in the form of a cross at the foot of the altar. It is gently and slowly created, one flower at a time. When the Spaniards arrived, the Indians related to the European cross as a symbol of their four directions.

By two-thirty in the morning the floral cross is finished and the singing prayers stop. We break and go outside to a star-filled sky. Coffee sweetened with honey is passed out in small earthen jugs. Then a basket filled with tamales is brought in. The tamales are meatless but spiced with diced jalapeños. They fill us and are delicious. We go back inside.

At four-thirty in the morning I begin to doze off. As I sit, my head drops and my whole body begins to plunge. Startled by my fast approach to the floor, I awaken and sit up. This happens again.

Throughout the vigil, since we arrived, fireworks have been going off into the night sky. In the morning I can still hear the whistling rockets and when we go outside I see the smoking trails above the trees exploding into the blue sky.

At one in the afternoon we eat: *Mole* with diced cactus, beans and tortillas. No forks, spoons or knives. Andrés tells everyone how Mexican restaurants in los Estados Unidos only serve two or three tortillas for each person. Everyone laughs as they eat their food with pieces of freshly made tortillas that never stop coming.

Afterwards, we prepare for a procession to the church atop a hill. About fifty men, women, children and elders return home for their ceremonial Aztec garments. Grey clouds begin to loom in the distance. The rockets continue to shoot up with their shrill whistles that end in explosions. The procession is difficult for three of us who carry Emilio's wheelchair up a rocky road to the church's front yard.

The Aztec dance troupe enters the church while Mass is being celebrated. Our procession prays for a good morning and leaves. I stay inside where the priest is angry, bitterly complaining about the Aztec dances. "It is nothing but a *pachanga!*" he raises his voice, "It has nothing to do with religion." He then complains about certain citizens of Tepetlixpa who have converted to the *Testigos de Jehovah.* Our procession is oblivious to the priest's insults. They believe in Christ and the Virgin, but see the Church is just an insensitive institution and nuisance. And in the background one hears the staccato of Aztec drums, mandolins, the scream of rockets and explosions in the sky.

Andrés leads the ceremonial dances in front of the Church. At the same time I notice from the top of the hill the Tepetlixpa municipal band marching through the pueblo on the way up to the Church.

The ceremonial dances last two hours and during the breaks the municipal brass band plays a number or two. Without communicating, the band and the Aztec dancers take turns. Andrés takes a break and sits on a rock wall next to me. I finally ask him about the fireworks. He looks at me refusing to answer. Then he says, "You have to feel it!"

I listen intently to the growing number of shrill whistles

and explosions. Then I begin to hear the reverberating echo of the explosions from the dark clouds. The echoes sound like thunder. The explosions have been transformed into thunder or have made the clouds thunder. A miracle, a mirage of sounds. The clouds are heavy, and they begin to thunder. But no rain.

We all return, chanting down the hill to the adobe room for closing prayers. The dark clouds cover us but still there is no rain.

At four-thirty in the afternoon, the vigil ends. We thank everyone, pack up the car and close the trunk as big drops of rain fall and raise tiny swirls of dust from the ground. "It never fails," explains Emilio with a smile. "Just as we leave, the rain arrives."

We leave, and I feel no cultural distance. We are one people separated only by space. Culture and time are not separated. We drive through the deep, green milpas. Andrés is exhausted and falls asleep. I too fall into a soft slumber. We talk no more. I understand more about maíz and passive resistance.

C/s

He Who Serves Two Masters Disappoints One ... or Both

"This question may bother you," began the radio interviewer in Mexico City, "but do you write as a Mexicano or...?"

The question trailed off but he didn't have to finish that one question forever asked of Chicanos by Mexicanos. "What exactly are you?"

The question was not only expected but welcomed, so the answer was quick and enthusiastic, *"Yo soy Mexicano!"* I answered, but added in Spanish, "And I am a *gabacho!* Culturally, I have as much of the Mexicano as I do of the gringo. I am as comfortable with the Mexican as a I am with the Anglo-American culture."

Never before had I claimed to be a gabacho or even thought of myself as one, much less proclaimed it in a live radio interview. Yet at that instant I found it necessary to emphasize and reaffirm my cultural and patriotic allegiance to the United States of America. Not to U.S. policy in *Latinoamérica* but to the United States of the people. I am the Southwest, I am tortillas and frijoles, but I am also hamburgers and hot dogs.

The Chicano Movement was an act of identity and self-determination. It was meant to dispel the notion of inferiority of *Mexicano-Norteamericanos*. It was a reaffirmation of our indigenous ancestry as well as our Mexican ancestry. But we never claimed to be gringos. On the contrary, we fought the yoke of the gringo oppressor while aspiring for equal opportunities.

We are both. We are "the vanquished, the victor," wrote Corky Gonzalez in his epic poem, "I am Joaquín." Poet José Montoya said it another way, "... the theys are us," and Pogo's famous line, "We have met the enemy and it is us," was all too applicable to the Mexican-American. Another friend said, "I'm Mexican by nature and American by nurture." We were caught on the razor sharp edge of two vastly different cultures, and in trying to identify with each side, while condemned by both sides, we denounced both and identified as a third alternative with a little and a lot from each side. We became Chicanos.

Born, razed and edgiekated on the border, I crossed the Rio Grande daily into *la madre patria*. It was the old world, returning to the past, nostalgic trips into day dreams of sights, sounds, street and kitchen odors. This is where grandmothers, aunts, uncles and cousins lived in Mexico. But through the brutal reality of childhood they opened our eyes to the fact that we were not Mexicanos. We were *pochos*, bastardized Mexicanos! A pocho, the

Spanish dictionary states, is spoiled fruit. If anyone was vilified more than the Chicano, it was the gringo. Then I was a Mexicano to them because they would tell me the sins of the Anglo-American character I was picking up, losing my Mexicanness.

Years later, while I was stationed in Spain, a few Spaniards would tell me of their bitter dislike of the Anglo-American. "I tell you this because you are not an Americano! You are a Mexicano! You're are not like them. You know the difference!" My silence was one of humorous bewilderement to be considered *más* Español than Americano.

As occasional trips take me back to Mexico I continue to hear the bickering and complaints about the Americanos. Finally, I told one Mexican friend that I was tired of hearing my *paisanos gringos* insulted. She was speechless as I explained my earlier comment, that culturally, I had assimilated much of the Anglo-American culture. Chicanos have the advantage of maintaining the best human values of both cultures.

Some people have always considered Chicanos gringos. Frank Del Olmo, the *Los Angeles Times* editorial writer, likes to tell about the time in Nicaragua when a *campesino* asked him if he was a gringo or not. Frank explained at length to the campesino that he was a Chicano. Then the campesino again asked him, "Well are you, or are you not a gringo?"

As relations between Mexicanos and Chicanos warm and grow each day, there is a tendency for Mexicanos to confuse what exactly a Chicano is. The word Chicano has caught on in Mexico.

According to Rodolfo de la Garza, University of Texas at Austin professor, Mexicans have begun to romanticize about Chicano history as they understand it through the movies and literature. De la Garza compares this to the Chicanos romanticization of Mexico during the Chicano movement.

More recently, the Mexican government and press have at times named all Mexicans residing in the United States as Chicanos. The documented and undocumented Mexican population in this country is enormous when it includes with Chicanos. Thirty million by the 21st Century? Our importance is critical to Mexico's future.

Mexico sees, or is blinded by, the potential lobby of both the Mexican residents in the United States and the actual United States-born citizens of Mexican ancestry, alias Mexican-Americans, Chicanos. But the Chicano now seems to be saying, *"Un momento!* Not so *rápido!* Don't take me for granted. I am a United States-born citizen."

If Mexico thinks we have sold out, consider the other half of the story. In this country, Chicanos are Mexico's biggest defenders. After the recent formation of a Mexican Commission on Human Rights along the border, the Commission quickly realized that Chicanos in the United States have long struggled for the rights of Mexican citizens in this country. What Chicanos do not necessarily support is the Mexican government or the ruling PRI party.

While we may defend and protect the United States national character in Mexico, we also defend and protect the Mexican national character in the United States. This may seem like a contradiction, but culturally we are tied to our mother country. "We are binational," says Luis Valdez. And ultimately we have but one political allegiance—Mexico. As the Spanish saying goes, "He who serves two masters, disappoints one or both."

That narrow border where I grew up has expanded and extended even to Alaska. Mexicanos and Chicanos live in greater numbers in the interior of the United States. Our bilingual, bicultural, binational experience is a form of schizophrenia, rich and poor, sun and shadow, between realism and surrealism. To live on the border is to inhabit two worlds, two cultures, and to accept both without diminishing the integrity of either.

C/s

Reasons to Celebrate
El Cinco de Mayo

The U.S. Civil War might have turned out very different had the French won the battle that *Cinco de Mayo,* 1862 in Puebla, Mexico. Had the French been victorious, they would have aided the South in the U.S. Civil War and our destiny might have been very different.

Justo Sierra, 1848–1912, a great Mexican writer and author of *The Political Revolution of the Mexican People* made this observation at the turn of the century.

In 1861, Mexico was bankrupt, owing staggering sums to Britain, Spain, France and the United States. Years earlier, the United States had offered to cover Mexico's debt in exchange for a mortgage on part of Mexico's territory. Having already lost half its territory to the United States, Mexico rejected the offer.

What kept the European powers from direct intervening in Mexico was the Monroe Doctrine of 1823, which prohibited Europe from interfering in this hemisphere.

But in the summer of 1861 the U.S. Civil War broke out and in October, France, Spain and England convened to sign the Covenant of London, agreeing to send troops to Mexico in sufficient numbers to secure payments. They solemnly added that this use of force was not for territorial gain or, ironically, to interfere in Mexico.

Spain and England sent the first bill-collecting expedition to Veracruz. Although the Europeans encountered no resistance and an agreement was reached, they didn't collect their money.

Meanwhile, France landed a sizable force, and the European intervention became exclusively French. On May 5, 1962, the French attacked Puebla, and a ragtag, poor and hungry, half Indian-Mexican army, under General Ignacio Zaragoza de Seguín, beat the better armed French forces, at that time the most powerful on earth. Zaragoza, ironically, was born in Goliad, Texas, when that state was under the Mexican flag.

The victory gave Mexico an electric current of patriotism and inspiration. It gave Mexico a soul of her own and national unity. This is perhaps one reason why el Cinco de Mayo is almost as important as September 16, Mexican Independence Day.

While the Cinco de Mayo battle raged, Robert E. Lee was winning battles for the South. Had France won at Puebla, it would have joined forces with the South and easily convinced England to help free the Southern ports of the Union blockade. Louisiana had at one time been French. France and England also wanted to halt U.S.

expansion into Latin America. Napoleon III also dreamed of establishing stronger ties between France and Mexico since both were Latin countries and in the process gave birth to the term "Latin America."

The victory at Puebla not only protected the integrity of Mexico but also that of the United States—"an involuntary service . . . of inestimable value," Justo Sierra wrote in *The Political Revolution of the Mexican People.*

A year later the French won several victories, paving the way for Napoleon III to send Maximilian, the unemployed Archduke of Austria, and his wife Carlota, to set up a monarchy in Mexico. But the Mexican resistance persisted and Washington continued to recognize the Benito Juarez government as the only legitimate one. At times, the Juarez government was situated in El Paso del Norte now renamed Ciudad Juarez and across from El Paso, Texas. At times the Juarez government had to go into temporary exile across the Rio Grande in Franklin, Texas, now named El Paso, Texas.

Maximilian and Carlota set up their court, wrote a book on court etiquette and reintroduced royal grandeur, first imported to Mexico City by Spain.

In 1865, the U.S. Civil War ended, and in 1866 armed resistance against the French occupation grew. The victorious U.S. Union army clamored for war against the French in Mexico. General Ulysses Grant declared it was necessary to aid the Republic of Mexico. Grant had already been to Mexico as part of the American invasion of 1847. For Mexico, the possibility of U.S. involvement was more frightening than the French presence. At U.S. urging, the French departed, but also because they had their own problems in Europe.

So the United States inadvertently repaid Mexico for its help in keeping the French from becoming allies of the Confederates.

But Maximilian would not abdicate his throne, declaring he was 100 percent Mexican, heart and soul. Besides, Napoleon had promised to stand by him. Carlota had already returned to France to hold Napoleon to his word. Napoleon reneged.

Maximilian remained in Mexico and bravely met his execution on June 19, 1867. Carlota became despondent and eventually went insane. She died in Belgium in 1922.

Mexico's second war of independence ended with 300,000 casualties.

How did France influence Mexico? Mexican law is based on the Napoleonic Code and Mexico's architecture was greatly influenced. Popular dances such as "La Varsoviana" are of French origin. Mexico's bread and pastries are of French origin. In Cuernavaca, the police are still called gendarmes. In Mexico City, *El Paseo de la Reforma* was Maximilian's idea of a direct route to his palace from the center of the city. It was modeled after the Champs-Elysees. (Contrary to popular belief, the French did not influence or institute *mariachis.*)

Had Mexico not won at Puebla, it is very possible that the South might have won the war and we might have had a different Mexico and a different United States. Thus we have every reason and right to celebrate. *Vive le diferens! Viva el Cinco de Mayo! Viva México!*

C/s

Childhood, Imagination and the Art Process

It was in a hot desert alley behind our El Paso home that I found small pieces of broken wood scattered throughout. I wasn't more than six years old when I picked up these fascinating pieces of jagged wood. One of them looked like the head of an axe and another like the handle. I put the pieces together, found a piece of wire and tied my axe together. With care, this axe would last for a game or two. I was so excited with my axe I ran inside the house to show Mamá. She turned from the stove, took the axe, studied it and smiled. I could hardly wait to run out and play with it when she asked if she could keep it? "Sí, Mamá." I answered, though I hated parting with my new toy.

We have all been there, when as children we created a

mountain from sand, a house from a box, a boat from half a nut shell, a tent from our bed covers or the fastest vehicle on earth from a skate and a board. Once, we were pilots on World War II flying fortresses made of wooden fruit boxes, and though we never left the ground we flew to the farthest reaches of our imagination. We constructed a world and a heaven of our own, fragile as our imagination. We turned dreams into reality. No toy in the world was more real and more thrilling than that created with our own hands, from our imagination.

But through the process of growing up, we forgot that world and now frown when children, bored with expensive toys, play with the boxes and wrappings that require more imagination. We justify video games as educational. If television and expensive toys weren't enough to rob our children of imagination and the creative process, most schools place little, if any, importance on art.

However, for writers, playwrights, *músicos,* actors, painters, *poetas,* sculptors, and other *artistas,* that ingenious imagination never left. Juan Rulfo, one of Mexico's greatest writers, acknowledged that it was his childhood memories that helped him capture the literary magic realism he is credited with having invented. Gabriela Mistral, the first Latin American writer to receive the Nobel prize for literature, began writing poetry as a young girl and never stopped. Pablo Picasso, one of this century's greatest painters, stated he forever tried to undo all he had ever learned about painting so as to return to a more original and rewarding imagination, uncluttered by standards and traditions. *Nicaragüense* Rubén Darío, who brought Spanish-language poetry into the twentieth century and modern times authored one of the most beautiful and nostalgic Spanish language poems about childhood, "*Juventud, divino tesoro, ya te vas para no volver ...*"— "Youth, divine treasure, you leave never to return."

Like the child, the artist begins with nothing. U.S. painter and teacher Robert Henri in *The Art Spirit* stated ". . . the life of an artist is a battle wherein great economy must be exercised. The kind of economy which will result in moments of purest freedom in spite of the world's exactions."

On another occasion, Henri taught artists to look at the world like children and not focus directly on one object. He recounts the story of a friend who takes his two boys to the circus for the first time and keeps telling them to "Look! Look!" But they were always looking the wrong way. The father was disappointed until that night he heard them telling their mother about the circus. Then he realized they had seen much more than he had.

Teaching how to look, Betty Edwards, professor of art and author of *Drawing on the Right Side of the Brain* teaches that anybody can draw if they use their intuitive side of the mind rather than the trained, analytical left side of the brain. The results have been impressive.

Like art imitating life, children imitate life through a fresh and innocent but sincere perspective. Art is a reflection and expression of life. Style, according to singer Roberta Flack, is sincerity with grace. A work of art is successful when accomplished in an original manner never experienced before.

As for my little wooden axe: My mother kept it for forty some years and when she passed away it was returned to me. I never played with it, but I now have it inside a glassed case as one of my first, and perhaps finest work of art. It can be categorized as found object art or assemblage art. I look at it and my imagination takes me back to a hot desert alley where perhaps a crucial seed was planted.

C/S

Piñatas

They don't make piñatas like they used to. There was a time when each piñata was made with individual art and craftsmanship. The colors were brighter and the shapes more geometric and less recognizable. They were also heavier because inside each one was a clay pot for the candy.

Today, the colors have faded, the craftsmanship is slipshod and they are made into every conceivable papier-maché shape from transformer toys to Batman and Bart Simpson. It was as inevitable as the law of supply and demand. The age of the classical piñata has come to pass.

Its history goes back to before the twelfth century when Marco Polo brought it to Italy from China, where it was used to celebrate the springtime harvest. In Italy it was called a *pignatta* and became a popular game with the nobility, which filled it with costly gifts. It then traveled to Spain, where it became part of the lenten traditions. The Sunday after Ash Wednesday became Piñata Sunday and the piñata was filled with candies.

In Mexico, there was already a similar tradition to celebrate the birth of the Aztec God Huitzilopochtli during the month of December. During the ceremonies, a feather-covered pot was filled with small treasures and hit with a stick so that its contents spilled at the feet of the idol. Thanks were given to Huitzilopochtli, who was responsible for the sun coming out every morning. The piñata represented evil and the children who destroyed it represented goodness.

Besides the enjoyment of this pastime, there are many other primary or secondary benefits. It is claimed to have therapeutic effect by releasing a child's aggression, frustration and anger on a dangling, inanimate object, though one must hit it while blindfolded.

There is also the "Piñata Syndrome," a theory advanced by Roberto P. Haro, a Chicano educator and administrator at San Jose State University, with the help of Herman Sillas, Chicano attorney, activist and troublemaker.

According to Haro, a piñata-buster is a risk-taker who seldom gets the goodies. He busts the system wide open for others, not necessarily for himself. "By the time the blindfold is removed, the best candy has been taken by the others. Only on rare occasions are the most desirable treats shared with the piñata-buster."

These piñata-busters or risk-takers are also known as "troublemakers" and shunned by others for not being "team players." Some are denied everything because they "went public" on sensitive issues. Like the piñata-busters, at best they get the *sobras*—leftovers. It is the classic case of the quiet and controllable "good Latinos" getting promoted at the expense of the risk-takers.

Though the piñata is a children's game, the metaphors and lessons to be learned are valuable to adults. In such a crowd you have all kinds of kids and parents and sometimes it's hard to tell them apart. There are adults who have as much fun as the kids, adults who after blindfolding the child turn them around so many times that the kids get dangerously dizzy if they don't first throw up their cake and ice cream. One end of the rope has to be securely tied to an object high enough that a tall person at the other end can swing the piñata over the child's head.

Fidgety little kids will press, push and shove each other as they turn, jump, and scratch, squeal, yell and cry trying to get in line to swing at the piñata. The littlest ones get priority against the Goliath piñata without a blindfold. They're tiny-tot cute and do little if any damage to the piñata as they swing all the way to the ground. But some show aggressive promise. The little leaguers are the most dangerous as they try to show off the crushing power of their swings.

And, there is always the danger of hitting another kid. Safety is of extreme importance when dealing with a crowd of little human candy vultures who jump in every time the piñata is struck. Upon hearing the thud and screams, the blindfolded hitter will begin to swing wildly. This is the most dangerous part of the game.

Gentle crowd control is essential when dealing with children oblivious to a wild swinging stick at the hands of a blindfolded kid. Police could get their basic training by dealing with children. As an experienced former kid and current parent I have witnessed and experienced harrowing piñata parties.

My friend, José Novoa, remembers a family of practical jokers in Guadalajara, México, who always had three piñatas at their parties. However, two of them would be booby-trapped. One would have dirt and the other water.

My most memorable piñata story happened when I was eight and my parents took us to seven-year-old Estela's birthday party in old Juarez, Mexico. The dirt patio was teeming with kids, music and noise while the parents and relatives clung to the surrounding adobe walls talking and drinking.

The birthday girl's father was a *policia*. He had come home early for the *fiesta* and was happy to be in his adobe castle, still wearing his uniform and gun. El Señor Flores joined his compadres to celebrate and toast his daughter's birthday. He felt proud, boastful and very much the macho in charge as the piñata was raised on the rope and dangled over the party. I was under the piñata, waiting for the line to form as other little kids jumped, ran, cried and screamed.

The next thing I remember was a loud "bang" and the piñata crashed down on my head. I was dazed by the heavy broken pot and thrown on the ground along with candy in fancy wrappers. Kids could have cared less if I was dead, as they picked the candy from my chest and under my head and then walked, jumped or tripped over me. My parents eventually rescued me from the scavenging mob of kids. I was all right but very angry.

El muy macho Señor Flores had pulled out his gun and shot the piñata in front of God, kids and parents. I don't recall what kind of commotion ensued from the parents but I remember the *policia pendejo* didn't even apologize. He just saw that I was okay and smiled snidley behind his fat mustache. In those days, piñatas were heavy and the earthen pot in the center was not easy to break. I still remember the sting in my hands when the stick hit a pot that refused to break. Today, they are made of nothing more than cardboard and papier-maché.

When I think of that childhood incident, it makes me feel like the Chicano version of William Tell's son, whose father shot an apple off the top of his head with a crossbow. Like my hands, that memory still stings.

C/s

Memories of
a Juarez Nightlife

Some news travels slow. On Sunday, November 27, 1988, Ciudad Juarez, Chihuahua, Mexico, began closing its bars as early as 11 p.m. It seem incredible to those of us who knew the wide-open town near the Rio Bravo, across from El Paso, Texas.

For millions of G.I.s who served at Fort Bliss and other military installations around the Southwest during World War II, the Korean War, the Vietnam War or peacetime, Juarez was their first introduction to a foreign country, to drinking, brothels and fiesta time.

Adolescent adventures abound in a Mexican-American grafitti style of life on the border. At the tender age of sixteen, young El Pasoans could discover Juarez, the wildest town south of Las Vegas. The shock of discovering a brothel and porn flicks was a bad dream for the innocent. High school football games and proms often ended in trips to Juarez, where puberty, a fake ID card and money would get you into any bar.

Naively, we bought cheap, cherry-flavored alcohol and snuck it past the U.S. customs officers at the bridge. As we grew older our tastes became more sophisticated, but we continued to smuggle the liquor in lowered 1950 Chevys and Fords. Today it would be extremely unadvisable to smuggle or taunt the customs officials like we used to.

Tijuana may have been more famous because of its proximity to Hollywood but Juarez was unique because of its desert mountains, international trolleys, quickie divorces and Pancho Villa's historic struggle with General John J. Pershing. Juarez's strip was born as a result of prohibition. To drink, Texans had only to cross the bridge. Even after prohibition, the state remained dry. Except for private clubs, only beer and wine was sold in El Paso bars.

Forget Gay Paree! Avenida Juarez was the Champs-Elysees complete with its own "Follies" and *El Lobby,* where the meanest dancers boogied through the '40s, rhythm-and-blued in the '50s and rocked through the '60s and '70s to "made in the USA" bands.

A block down from El Lobby was Carlos' Bar, a.k.a. The Mex-Tex, where the best *mariachis* played sad *corridos,* ballads, wild polkas or classic symphony pieces. Some argued that the mariachis at the San Luis Bar down the street were much better. They had a mariachi singer with such a great voice that opera lovers came to hear him sing corridos—until a group of civic-minded El Paso women sponsored his study of opera and he was never heard from in Juarez again.

During the wild and crazy '50s, people spilled from the sidewalks along the Avenida Juarez drinking from bottles of José Cuervo or Bacardi, meeting strangers as friends, long-forgotten amigos, single women and exchanging toasts. New Year's and football victories were celebrated in the streets. Juarez was Mardi Gras everyday of the year.

It was in the '50s that Juarez achieved international acclaim for its "quickie" divorce laws. The internationally rich and famous, from Elizabeth Taylor to Marilyn Monroe, had only to take a quick trip to El Paso to shed so many pounds of ugly husbands and thousands of dollars in a matter of minutes. The end of quickie divorces came on October 10, 1970, as Mexico sought a better image. Right up to that date, men swarmed the hotels and bars looking for women celebrating their new-found freedom.

In the New Yorker Bar with its 1920s Mexican tiled decor, I was arrested and jailed for having punched a young drunk who had insulted me. My supposed friends went to bail me out only to run across some girls and forget about me. In jail, I ran across an uncle, who was serving time for shooting and killing two ex-mayors of Juarez at the Mint Bar, a few feet from the International Santa Fe Bridge. After being wounded and lying on his back, Mexico's champion target shooter had pulled out his 45. caliber with his left hand and shot them dead in self-defense. He then tried a run to the bridge but was captured halfway across. He was brought back to trial and a seven-year sentence while the *pueblo,* the people, turned him into a hero with ballads, poems and essays. Through their power, wealth, and arrogance, the two ex-mayors had abused and robbed across the state of Chihuahua for years.

Crossing the International Santa Fe Bridge back to El Paso was a ritualistic process. First you paid the toll of three pennies, then you passed on to a U.S. Customs officer who first asked for declaration of citizenship and then what kinds of products you were bringing into the country. Fruits, plants and meats were strictly forbidden. Delicious Mexican avocados could be passed if the big seed was taken out.

My father recalled those days when the bridge was wooden and the banks were lined with old Alamo trees from which Pancho Villa hung many men. Even earlier, my grandmother recalled the boats, the rafts, and the floods. In those days before the turn of the century the river was untamed and wild. My aunt, *tía* Elena inherited valuable Mexican property on land that had shifted to the U.S. side when the river had changed course. She gave up hope of ever receiving compensation for her property and so she threw away her property title—only to live through the day when the U.S. Government agreed to settle the Chamizal land dispute with Mexico and compensated those who had lost their lands.

I still recall the river banks lined with trees and wild shrubs. But they obstructed the *Migra's* vigilante ways and so the river was defoliated. In the '50s, Mexican boys poised themselves below the bridge on the river bed, with long poles in their hands. At the top end of the poles were cardboard cones to catch coins pitched by *turistas*. Hundreds of pennies, nickels, dimes and dreams were lost in the muddy current.

In Juarez, bars that never closed encouraged drinking marathons. Some started on Friday night in El Paso, closing up El Paso at midnight, driving a few miles into

New Mexico where they closed at two, then on to Juarez, where the bars never closed. Then it was back to open up El Paso's bars, close them, close New Mexico and return to Juarez. The marathon's grand finale would take place Sunday afternoon at the Monumental Bull Ring in Juarez, sitting on the cheap, sunny side with a pail of Cruz Blanca beer. Then it was back to El Paso only to pass out under some freeway bridge.

Behind the bright lights district in dark streets and alleys were the *Maestro* Bars where Mexican blue collar workers relaxed. Once in a while Tarahumara Indians would venture into a bar only to be refused service. From bar to bar, a boy escorted his blind father who played the guitar, sang and collected pesos and quarters for haunting melodies of love gone sour. Old women selling flowers, dancing dogs and men with electric shock boxes made their way from bar to bar. These electric shock boxes had two cables that ended with two steel rods to be held in each hand. An electric current would then be turned on and increased until the rods were dropped.

There was the famous Tommy's Bar where my uncle, Francisco Morales invented the most popular drink of all time, the Margarita. There was the Manhattan Bar, with its thousand-drink repertoire and a seven piece marimba band.

Curley's Bar began as a high-class soft music lounge. Then Curley's changed owners and it was named the Noa Noa where young Mexican bands came to imitate the best rock hits in mimicked english. The Noa Noa was made famous by Mexican composer and singer Juan Gabriel, born in Juarez and influenced by El Paso radio pop music.

Some El Paso high schools claimed their own bar. Such

was Fred's Rainbow Bar, where El Paso High and Cathedral High schoolers hung out. There we drank sweet mixed drinks or cheap Corona and Cruz Blanca beer along with the delicious Mexican sandwiches we called "cancer sandwiches" because eating Avenida Juarez street food was not advisable.

The Submarine, the Caverns and so many other bars all had first-rate bartenders who personally catered to their clients and became friends, confidants and counselors: "Stay in school, go to college." The sidewalks were lined with hundreds *of curio* stores and stalls selling everything from beautiful silver and gold jewelry to black velvet paintings and "horse shit" cigarettes. Shoeshines went for a dime, while artists and pre-Polaroid photographers stalked vain customers who took their photographs and then ran to develop the photos that would soon turn a sepia color. Cheating husbands and wives kept their distance from popular hangouts and photographers.

Cabdrivers forever wanted to take you to Irma's or Cherry Hill, mansions of ill repute with pseudo-Greek plaster of paris imitations of Corinthian columns and Venus sculptures.

Once, a friend we called Baby was robbed by a cabdriver in Juarez. The next night, Baby had a friend hire the same cabdriver to bring him back to El Paso. Once in El Paso, Baby jumped into the cab and at gunpoint forced the driver to a deserted mountain road overlooking the bright lights of both cities. There he was left naked and his cab keys thrown into a brush-filled arroyo.

Because of Juarez, El Paso was a natural convention city for everyone from LULAC, the League of United Latin American Citizens, and the GI Forum to firemen, barber shop quartets, Sun Bowl football teams, fans and the ever faithful turistas.

But that was long ago. The death of Juarez nightlife began with the end of quickie divorces in 1970.

Meanwhile, El Paso, like the rest of Texas, was as dry as a bone in the desert, although bars could serve beer and wine. Then private clubs began serving liquor by the drink and they proliferated. The drought was officially drenched with the passage of a liquor-by-the-drink Texas Law in 1969.

The nightlife in Juarez had already begun to change. Few El Pasoans crossed over for fear of Mexican police and their *mordidas*—bribes—or the bridge delays and closings that ran anywhere from one hour to several days depending on the time of day, season, U.S. customs searches and Mexico's political climate.

The statewide order to close bars early came from Chihuahua Governor Fernando Baeza as a crime prevention measure. The cost of crime was more than the income from the night life industry. *Maquiladoras,* U.S. assembly plants, have replaced the Juarez night establishments as its main industry. But I'll always have memories of when we helped build that nightlife industry.

C/s

La Cate

In 1955, in El Paso's Cathedral Catholic Boys' High School, the freshman class sat in rapt attention as Brother Alphonsus informed us about the new high school facility we would graduate from. But 1959 came, and my class graduated from the same poor facility. Thirty-two years later, 1991, *La Cate,* as it is known to students and alumni, continues to graduate students from the same facility. In 1990, 70 percent of its 366 students were Chicanos and came from every section of the city, including eleven students from Juarez, Mexico.

But despite its reputation as the poorest high school in El Paso, where the median income in 1992 is $11,000, Cathedral's academic reputation has grown from a local to a national level.

Over the past four years, 98 percent of its graduates have been accepted to universities across the country. In 1990 that figure hit and has stayed at 100 percent. All 82 of its graduates attend colleges and universities from the local University of Texas at El Paso to Stanford, Harvard, Duke, Cornell, Princeton, Notre Dame, Georgetown, Trinity and others. The 82 seniors garnered a total of 55 scholarships worth more than $1 million dollars.

Steve Ramirez, 1989 graduate, received the prestigious AT&T Scholarship. That's the "cadillac" of scholarships. Only 15 are awarded nationally and they pay four years of tuition, books, provide a summer job, trips home, and a guaranteed job after graduation. That was the second AT&T Scholarship received by a Cathedral graduate.

As a barometer of its success, in 1989, the El Paso High School system, with its ten schools, had nine top scorers in the Scholastic Aptitude Test while Cathedral alone had four.

La Cate is not an elitist preppie school. Yet it approximates the success at Andover, Phillips Academy, or Exeter. Principal Brother Stephen Furches states, ". . . one third of our students are top-notch, but the other third are average kids who work hard."

Victor Miramontes, an associate with the Henry Cisneros Asset Management Company in San Antonio and a member of the Cathedral High School Board of Trustees, graduated in 1970 and is also a Stanford University graduate. Miramontes is convinced the reason is not because of the self-selection process but because it has a three-legged support system. "You have the kids, parents and faculty."

I can remember the Sunday night Bingo games thirty years ago. Mothers selling tacos and fathers selling beer while the students helped set up the tables, take them down and clean up.

Miramontes believes the lack of money is part of La Cate's success. "Ten million dollars would hurt Cathedral's success. The key lies in having to hustle for a living. There's a sense of camaraderie." The Parent-Teacher Association is very important to help supplement school expenses.

As high as one third of the students are first time college-bound in their families. Five to ten percent are the first in their families to graduate from high school. A former Cathedral High graduate, Brother Oscar Santaella, now principal of St. Michael's High School in Santa Fe, had this perspective on the success of his alma mater:

After transferring from a public high school to Cathedral "... we were taught church values, dedication, and that everyone has a God-given ability. I never saw that at the public high school I attended."

In 1981 he returned to his alma mater as a faculty member. Brother Santaella found the same values, enthusiasm and drive, "I never listened to students who said, 'I can't do it.'"

Brother Oscar Santaella became assistant principal and then principal. He continued to instill the same values and educational techniques he received as a student and accepted no less from his charges.

Bobby O'Dell, a 1989 graduate, found his four years at Cathedral fulfilling and difficult, "The curriculum is one of the toughest," he says. "At other schools, students get to choose their courses. At Cathedral the only thing we choose are electives."

It hasn't changed since I graduated thirty years ago. My

only two electives were typing and mechanical drawing. No courses in creative writing or art were offered then. Somehow I still became a writer and artist.

In such an atmosphere of scholastic pressure, discipline is essential. Thirty-two years ago it was normal for a Christian Brother to punch, paddle or slap a student. Such harsh discipline is gone. "Today there is more inter-personal dialogue and psychology. Kids know their legal rights, and there's always the fear of litigation," says Brother Santealla.

In football, La Cate's team could probably enter the *Guiness Book of World Records* for the most games lost. One of the years when I was attending, our best season was five-five, five lost at home and five lost on the road. But in basketball the school has garnered the state title in the Texas Catholic Intercollegiate playoffs several times. And its debate teams are formidable in competition.

Cathedral graduates seem to do well in later life. In 1955, the mayor of El Paso was Raymond Tellez, a Cathe-dral graduate while across the border, the mayor of Ciu-dad Juarez was René Mascareñas, Tellez's friend and classmate. Mayor Tellez was eventually appointed U.S. ambassador to Costa Rica by President John F. Kennedy. Mascareñas is now a writer. Other graduates since then have become accomplished professionals and leaders in the corporate, governmental and educational fields.

The same sixty-six-year-old brown brick school that graduated those students continues to produce successful young men. According to students, the only thing holding up this Catholic private high school are the many coats of paint. The neighborhood, once a middle-class area, is now a low-income barrio. However, things are "supposed" to change. La Cate was to add a new facility on an adjoining parking lot. An adjoining city block has now been purchased. Considering the broken promises in the past, I will believe it only after I see it. But it doesn't really matter, as long as they keep providing a quality education.

C/S

The Last Supper
of Chicano Heroes

In 1988, I polled 100 Chicano students at Stanford University and 100 Chicano activists from the late 1960s to find out whom they considered the top thirteen Chicano heroes.

The idea arose from a mural that I was designing on the mythology and history of maíz, corn. I had intended to depict the Last Supper; Christ and his twelve apostles were to be portrayed eating tortillas, tamales and tequila instead of bread and wine. I dropped that idea when some students expressed dismay at my mixing humor with religion. That's when I decided to replace the religious figures with thirteen Chicano heroes. The mural, now finished, is in the dining hall of Casa Zapata, the Chicano-theme student residence at Stanford University.

The survey was received positively and as a novelty, with a 70 percent return.

The final thirteen Chicano heroes reflected the choice of the older activists because their votes were concentrated on a smaller group of heroes who had played important parts in the Chicano movement as activists or symbolic historical figures. The students were more inclusive and offered a total of 240 hero candidates.

The selection process brought into question the very definition of a hero or heroine as a mythical, historical, symbolic, military or popular cultural figure.

The first historical Chicano hero, according to some, was General Ignacio Zaragoza, born in Seguín, Texas, when Texas was part of Mexico. Zaragoza rose to command the ragtag Mexican army that defeated the French in Puebla on Cinco de Mayo, 1862. At that time, the French army of Napoleon III was the most powerful in the world. But Zaragoza did not make the final list. Nonetheless, he does stand behind the seated thirteen. One who did was a man who preceeded him both in time and in popular lore, the California rebel Joaquín Murrieta.

Three Chicanos who started their careers together made the list: Cesar Chavez, Dolores Huerta and Luis Valdez.

La Virgen de Guadalupe, patroness of Mexico, received enough votes to sit at the table but out of respect occupies a loftier place above the Chicano Last Supper. In a history mobbed with *machos,* there was a sincere effort to vote not only for women like Frida Kahlo and the poet Sor Juana Inez de la Cruz but also for mothers and grandmothers.

Not all the heroes had to be Chicano—that is, of Mexican ancestry; thus Argentine-born, Cuban hero Ernesto

"El Che" Guevara made the list. The martyred Che, a strong symbol during the Chicano Movement of the late sixties occupies the central position because he was the most Christ-like with his beard, revolutionary idealism and martyrdom. At his side is an earlier Mexican revolutionary, Emiliano Zapata.

Dr. Martin Luther King, Jr. was another non-Chicano who made the last supper. The late president John F. Kennedy also received some votes but not enough to sit at the table. He is in the background, along with General Zaragoza and others who did not make the final list.

Carlos Santana, who helped revolutionize North American music with Latino sounds stands and serenades the chosen thirteen.

Death received enough votes to stand behind the lucky thirteen. *La muerte,* so popular in Mexico, is a heroine, a great avenger and saviour from *la vida.*

One student voted for Juan Valdez of the television coffee commercial, José Cuervo tequila, Speedy Gonzalez, Señor Don Gato, Julio Iglesias, Pedro the Mexican Jumping Bean, Tattoo from Fantasy Island, Chiquita Banana, Menudo and Zorro the Gay Blade. This list was at once humorous and revealing about how Latinos are sometimes perceived through stereotypes and media stars.

Chicano heroes have always been an elusive lot. Mexicanos and Chicanos have traditionally frowned on the North American individualism that Alexis de Tocqueville described more than a century ago. Most of Mexico's national heroes were martyrs, having died in service to the people—from Miguel Hidalgo, father of Mexican Independence, who was excommunicated and executed, to revolutionary heroes Francisco Villa and Emiliano Zapata, who were ambushed and assasinated.

In the survey, the group-oriented focus came through time and again in votes for mothers, fathers, grandparents, Vietnam veterans, *braceros, campesinos* and *pachucos*. But it was best expressed by a student, who chose as his heroes, "all the people who died, scrubbed floors, wept, and fought so that I could be here at Stanford."

THE TOP THIRTEEN CHICANO HEROES

1. Cesar Chavez—Founder and president of the United Farm Workers Union.
2. Emiliano Zapata—Mexican revolutionary hero.
3. Dolores Huerta—Founder and vice president of the United Farm Workers.
4. Frida Kahlo—Mexican painter, wife of Mexican muralist Diego Rivera.
5. Luis Valdez—Founder of *El Teatro Campesino*, playwright and director of films such as *La Bamba* and *Zoot Suit*.
6. Ernesto "El Che" Guevarra—Argentine-born hero of the Cuban revolution.
7. Joaquin Murrieta—Young Californio rebel/ bandit, fought against yankees.
8. Tomás Rivera—Chicano educator and writer.
9. Sor Juana Inez de la Cruz—fifteenth-century Mexican nun, poet, early feminist.
10. Dr. Martin Luther King, Jr.—Civil Rights leader who supported the farmworkers and inspired the Chicano movement.

11. Benito Juarez—Mexican President, liberator. Contemporary of Abraham Lincoln.
12. Ricardo Flores Magón—Mexican revolutionary, writer and intellectual.
13. Ernesto Galarza—Early Chicano activist, writer, poet and Stanford graduate.

C/s

Beggars and *Pordioseros*

In this land of downtowns where tall buildings scrape the sky with opulence, men still beg beneath them. From the shadows of these majestic wonders, men beg for handouts, a meal, a cup of coffee.

We know them well, some of us. They have always been there whether we liked them or not. I have never grown accustomed to them. They tug at my conscience and guilt, reminders of my comforts and the injustice.

I remember them as a young child growing up on the border. On Christmas mornings, after opening our gifts, our parents packed their children into an old 1940 green Pontiac, crossed the Rio Grande and had us give clothing, food and toys to the poor children and women huddled against the cold doors of closed stores. It was an admirable lesson in charity from parents with six children living on the salary of a janitor. The reason had been whispered once in the middle of the night. In our one bedroom home, my father had told my mother, "These children will never know the poverty that I knew."

Despite these poignant lessons I grew accustomed to beggars in Mexico. In my arrogant adolescence I would point them to the nearest church tower.

In Mexico they are called *pordioseros,* literally meaning "for-God's-sakers." Many *turistas* are devastated when they first discover pordioseros. In this country, "beggars" is a word that screeches like chalk on our conscience so they are better known as panhandlers.

In Mexico, men don't beg. It's usually women and small children. But in this country, generally speaking, men beg but women do not. Is it because this country provides more services and benefits for women than for men? Mexico barely provides services for destitute women and children and none for men. There are many cultural and social reasons for this difference. I am not a social anthropologist, but I am fascinated with the cultural aspects found in literature.

Until *Don Quixote De La Mancha* by Miguel Cervantes was published in 1605, the most popular book in the Spanish language had been, *La Vida de Lazarillo de Tormes,* author unknown, though some attribute it to Cervantes. This picaresque novel was about a young boy named Lazarillo, diminutive of Lázaro, which comes from "lacerated," victimized. The word "picaresque" was born into literature through this novel. Lazarillo was a rogue, a vagabond, trying to etch out a living in picaresque ways and worked as a servant for more masters than one can count.

In one episode, Lazarillo works for a seemingly wealthy Spanish master. This well-dressed gentleman walks about the *pueblo* with a gold toothpick in his mouth and feigns a full and satisfied stomach. But eventually he hurries home to see what Lazarillo has been able to scrape up from his forays about town. The servant begs and feeds the master.

This demonstrates just how important social appearance is to the Spaniard. During my three years in Spain, from 1961 to 1964, I never saw a beggar. For one, General Francisco Franco would not permit them. I've returned to my grandmother country a few times since then only to discover them a nuisance outside the Prado Museum. But they were gypsy women, not full-blooded Spaniards.

Ernest Hemingway, whose love for Spanish culture was total, explained this Iberian character trait in a short story entitled "The Capital of the World." In the story, three Madrid bullfighters are described by Hemingway: "It is necessary for a bullfighter to give the appearance, if not of prosperity, at least of respectablity, since decorum and dignity rank above courage as the virtues most highly prized in Spain. . . ." This trait was brought over to Latin America.

Is this the reason Latino men in this country and Latin America do not beg? In Mexico you will find destitute men spitting out flames of fire from their mouths, dancing in Aztec costume for a handout, cleaning car windows on busy street corners, or selling miscellaneous trinkets, always providing a service, no matter how minimal, instead of begging. The most poignant and impressive of these working men that I have come across was a young Spanish poet in downtown Madrid. At an outside cafe, the young poet courteously approached each table to give photocopies of his poetry for whatever coins the person would drop in his palm.

There are high numbers of Chicao and Latino men incarcerated for theft, robbery and drug dealing; there are more of them in prison than in universities. Are those criminal alternatives less painful to Latinos than the cultural taboo against begging? Social banditry has been described as an outlet, unlawful as it is, for those who have no other recourse to making a living within society.

As in *Lazarillo de Tormes,* there will always be those poor Latinos of proud Hispanic blood we call *maestros,* though they may be down in their luck. One such man walked into a Spanish tavern in Mexico City. He must have been in his sixties with a head of silver-tousled hair. His walk was painful, half dragging his feet but with a dignity and air not in keeping with his growth of beard and soiled clothes. Thirsty and tired, he approached the bar and asked the bartender for a glass of water. The bartender interrupted his conversation with another customer, took a tall glass and filled it with cool, crystal-clear water. Then he handed the glass to the man as if it were a glass of cold beer. The old man took the glass, raised it, and thanked him as if in a toast. Then he turned around and toasted everyone at the bar. Some turned and acknowledged the toast with a nod of the head. The old man then raised the glass of water and with great aplomb and speed, emptied the thirst-quenching water into his mouth. He then put the glass down and after thanking the bartender, walked to the end of the bar next to the door and requested permission to leave, *"Con su amable permiso,"* he said. *"Es propio,"* answered one of the men at the bar, "It is proper." The old man bowed and walked away with the dying sun on his silver hair.

C/S

Mando, La Luz and Esmelta

The wallet-size photograph is sepia colored, fading fast and ragged around the edges. It dates back to the mid-sixties when the impact of the Vietnam War was tearing apart the United States.

The photo was taken in Juarez, Mexico, by a free-lance photographer who roamed from bar to bar, documenting *amistades* and illicit love affairs. But this photograph showed two *carnales,* the Limón brothers, Armando and Angel, totally inebriated at the Mex-Tex Bar. They sit at a small rickety wooden table overspilling with empty bottles of Dos Equis and glasses.

Mando, twenty, is passed out, his head rests on the table, right arm over his head and the left arm dangling. His brother Angel, two years younger, is still half-conscious, on the verge of falling forward, one elbow on the table and his eye-lids half-closed. This is their last blast together, Mando's going away party. "Yeah, *ese!*" Mando said, "When I come back from Nam I'm gonna go to college and major in engineering. I like being an aircraft mechanic and I'm better off in the Navy, *ese!* Two more years for volunteering but at least I'm not with the Army in the middle of some damn rice paddy."

His *carnalito* kept silent in a *chingón* sort of way. The *bato* weighed just under 100 pounds soaking wet and he didn't measure past five feet three inches. You could tell Limoncito was tough just by looking at him. But if you looked too long he might inquire, "Whatta you loo ... king at, *ese?* The other batos called him Limoncito, which is Little Lemon in *totacho*—English. That was up until the time we started calling him "La Luz!" When we called him "La Luz!" we would say it dramatically, like a heavy duty pachuco would whisper it: "Laahh Looooz!"

The way Limoncito got baptized as La Luz was from a real happening. Limoncito was riding low shotgun in Merch's car one Saturday night. They were the best of *camaradas* although Merch was a six-foot, 250-pound-Chicano. Merch was driving and yakking away about who and what, this and that. Limoncito sat slumped shotgun taking it all in and looking ahead. The green traffic light up ahead turned to yellow. Limoncito noticed that Merch was not slowing down. And Limoncito was not one to yell because he never raised his voice. He just whispered in a gruff sort of way because he had a high-pitched voice so in order to sound tough he always spoke in a gruff whisper. So Limoncito tried to get Merch's attention by whispering "La luuuz!" But Merch kept talking, oblivious to the approaching yellow light and intersection. Limoncito again whispered loudly "La luuuuuuz!" but there was no response from Merch. Limoncito finally had to sit up, pointed towards the light, jabbed the air with his finger and as loud as he could,whispered, "Laaaaaaa Luuuuuuuuuuuz!" With burnt rubber, Merch was able to stop on time and lived to tell all the other batos the story. And so Limoncito became known as "La Luz!"

Mando and La Luz were from Smeltertown, better known as Esmelta, Smelda, Melda or Imelda, depending on how one thought it sounded better. It's population couldn't have been over 500 Mexican-American working class souls, the salt of the earth. The town was more of a barrio located just up the Río Grande from El Chuco, and across the highway from Esmelta was ASARCO, the American Smelting and Refining Company. Esmelta was bad if you misbehaved. Food found out the hard way.

Food was Freddy's nickname. It came about because Freddy painted cartoons and caricature posters of people and signed his posters "Fred." One time, he did a cartoon of Texas Western College coach Don Haskins. The Coach misread Freddy's signature and asked, "Who's this guy named Food?"

Besides women, whom he found irresistible after a few drinks, Food had two other loves, drawing cartoons and drinking beer. He combined the two and sold his cartoons around the bars in El Chuco, for hard cash or pitchers of beer. But once he started drinking, there was no return.

One Friday night, Food went to a party in Esmelta with La Luz, got wiped out, misbehaved and then had the day lights beat out of him by some unknown guy from Esmelta.

The next night he called me and said, "Let's go catch a flick at the Trail Drive-In, *ese.*"

"Orale!" I answered, "I'll pick you up at seven o'clock."

It was a dark moonless night when I picked him up and drove out of his neighborhood. We stopped at a traffic light and he was so quiet I turned to see him. Food's face was a bloody, black and blue mess. He was bad, bad, bad. They must've kicked his face. Food looked horrible. So much so that I laughed. It was unreal in a painfully funny way.

Food didn't say anything. He was hurting physically and spiritually. He couldn't remember what had happened. At the movies, in the middle of the movie, in the middle of a love scene, he would howl like a wounded coyote at the moonless night. He was hurting so bad he wanted to cry.

Esmelta was bad if you didn't behave. The Limón brothers were cool as long as you didn't mess with them. La Luz couldn't remember what had happend to Food, either. It was worse than the time he had tried to pick up on a cop's wife at the Mex-Tex in J Town. The cop had bruised him bad.

Yet, one couldn't help but mess with La Luz. He was tiny and acted so bad, like a Chicano Humphrey Bogart. He didn't take too kindly to *la cábula,* the taunts and teases.

The way we got to know the Limón brothers was through the Town Lounge where we hung out drinking pitchers of beer, shooting pool and, teasing each other. Mando and La Luz worked next door at a Photo Developing business so they always stopped by for a cold one after hours or during coffee break. And Mando joined the Navy when the draft began breathing down his neck. Everybody was sweating the draft back then, in the middle of all the blood, guts and gore on living color television. So all our friends were going to college except for Mando and La Luz. Mando didn't consider college an option so he laughed off such suggestions. But when Mando returned from boot camp and aircraft mechanic school, there he was talking about college, his future and career.

The night he got drunk with La Luz was the last time we saw Mando. The Navy assigned him to the Enterprise, the nuclear aircraft carrier. It went out to sea, off the coast of Vietnam from where fighter jets flew bombing missions back and forth from the Enterprise. Finally one day a jet fighter crash landed on the deck.

From what we heard, Mando was safe, until he ran out to help extinguish the flames or rescue some of the injured sailors. That's when the fuel ran across the runway, caught fire and engulfed everyone on the burning deck. Mando was given last rites and didn't last very long after that. I had already left El Chuco and someone sent me his picture and obituary from the *El Chuco Herald Post*. He looked like such a young Chicano kid fighting an old gringo's war.

La Luz was heartbroken. You had never seen two closer friends, much less brothers. They respected each other, laughed together and drank together.

At the funeral La Luz wore a black suit and loud raspberry colored shirt. After the funeral, he stopped by the Town Lounge. Savage saw him and said, "Hey, *ese!* You look like a strawberry in a black cave!"

La Luz got very angry and in his sadness whispered, "I'm gonna have to go back to my old ways." That meant carrying his *filero* and being mean. La Luz stopped going to the Town Lounge. The last time I saw him was the week he visited Southern Califas, which he found terribly cold. All he had brought on his trip were T-shirts and short sleeves. It seemed like all he did was stand outside a Long Beach house on Ocean Boulevard drinking beer with us, one hand in his pocket and shivering. I teased him and one morning at six o'clock, as I was readying to go to work, we ran into each other in the bathroom. It was chilly and he whispered, "Don't tell me it isn't cold now."

La Luz went back to El Chuco, to his old ways, and one day he was thrown from a speeding car on Interstate 10. Mando and La Luz disappeared along with Smeltertown. The sulphur fumes from ASARCO had claimed too many Chicanitos lives so Smeltertown was razed and all that was left were the walls of the church and the street signs with the names of World War II Chicano heroes, like Willie Martinez. They stayed up for a while and then also disappeared. And once I looked for Mando's name on the Vietnam War Memorial in Washington, D.C., but he wasn't there either. They all disappeared, Mando, La Luz and Esmelta.

C/s

The Desert

Our canteens were empty when two friends and my brother and I realized how lost we were in the hot, 100-plus degree dry desert just north of El Paso. According to the sun's position, it was approximately two o'clock in the afternoon. In our pre teens, watches and wallets were a nuisance. We had hiked north and then turned west, expecting to get to the highway. Two hours later we were still walking without seeing any sign of civilization. The jagged rocks and yucca were begining to prick our shins and feet. Tired and thirsty, we trudged up and down one hill after another expecting to see a highway or the Río Grande.

We stopped to rest in the shade of a deep dry arroyo without saying much to each other. It was still too early to worry. The cool gulch was refreshing and quiet except for the deafening buzz of a fly. I lay on the cool bed of sand and tried to imagine earlier times when Apaches crossed those parts. I had yet to run across an arrowhead or bones but anything was possible. From time to time, the local newspaper carried stories about ancient wheels, crucifixes and bones. All we had stumbled on was shriveled dry wood, Yuccas, Ocotillos, Gobernadoras, Mesquite trees, dry arroyos, the dry carcass of a coyote and a rattlesnake's fragile translucent skin shed around a Mesquite tree. From time to time, a lizard would dart across our paths.

Through centuries of August rainfalls, the rushing waters had cut a deep arroyo and smoothly carved the rocks into boulders and pebbles. It was a dormant arroyo that turned into a ruthless river during the August "monsoon rains." Prefaced by the ominous clashing of Rocky Mountain thunder and rolling purple clouds, the rain from the mountains ran down to the Río like a flash flood. The waters also formed temporary lagoons in the desert and during September frogs would burrow from their dormant shells to serenade the coming of Fall.

After a half-hour rest in the arroyo we continued our hike west facing a beating hot sun. Our collective thirst and fear was growing stronger. At the bottom of one hill we saw in the distance a sprawling ranch house with a green lawn and a road. We ran down knowing that the green grass equaled a hose equaled water. Just like the cavalry would have done a century earlier we drenched our mouths with running water and then our heads, but not before letting the runnning water cool the hot hose.

The desert was our playground in days when cowboy movies were the rage and television was still unborn. We played cowboys but never Indians out of an unspoken treaty.

We loved the desert. It wasn't foreboding and hostile like a dark forest. It wasn't a forbidden wasteland but an open world with an awesome sky filled with brilliant night diamonds. The wind, sand and sun were tempests in a sea of desert.

Only one seventh of the earth is arid landscape. Contrary to what six sevenths of the world says, we were fortunate to learn to live in a desert climate. Most arid regions lie in the Tropic of Cancer, a narrow belt above the Equator or in the Tropic of Capricorn, below the Equator. There are twelve major deserts including our own North American desert which measures 500,000 square miles— almost twice the size of Texas. It encompasses the southwestern United States and northwestern Mexico. This great North American desert is made up of the Great Basin, the Mojave, the Sonoran and the Chihuahuan deserts.

But because of our interstate highways, modern transportation, canal systems, deep water wells, expanding cities and the modern convenience of air conditioning, our desert has virtually disappeared. Today the Sun Belt is the most rapidly growing part of this country. Only those who fall victim to the harsh realities of borders and racism remind us of the desert.

Someday there will be a monument to the men who were locked and abandoned in a suffocating railroad freight car. Someday there will be a monument to the men and women who sought to sneak across an unforgiving North American desert thinking perfume or urine would quench their thirst. Someday there will be a statue of liberty facing south that will characterize their dream not as greed but as escape from hunger and thirst for life and freedom.

The North American desert has a longer history in Mexico than in the United States. The *conquistadores* conquered the south of Mexico and soon set out in search of more wealth, including the seven cities of Cibola. That was greed.

They not only found the desert difficult to conquer but Mexico eventually lost the desert land to the "Manifest Destiny" of the United States. Not only was the desert difficult, but so were its indigenous people. The Spanish conquest of the Mayas and Aztecas was relatively easy. The Apaches and Yaquis, on the other hand, like many of the Plains Indians, fought more tenaciously and for many more years. In 1885, Geronimo and a band of 21 Apaches eluded 5,000 U.S. troops for almost ten months. Lacking supplies, they finally surrendered to General Crook in March of 1886, only to escape two nights later.

For Mexico, the northern desert has always been a refuge. Miguel Hidalgo, Father of Mexican Independence, sought exile in the North only to be captured and executed by the Spanish in Chihuahua. When Mexico was losing the war against France, Benito Juarez retreated to the northern desert. The Mexican Revolution of 1910 began in the desert state of Chihuahua, and its most famous son, Pancho Villa, was one of its most illustrious field generals. Villa successfully eluded capture in the desert by one of this country's most respected field commanders, General John J. Pershing.

Desert people have a pride and dignity coupled with incomparable survival skills. For Apaches a pebble under the tongue was enough to prevent dehydration when water holes were dry or far apart. Without deep oceans, trees, jungles or forests to hide the horizons, there is a clarity of vision. Inhabitants of the desert are not mad and ferocious as the Apaches and even Arabs have been stereotyped. In the loneliness of the desert people meditate, just as Christ did fasting in the desert for 40 days and 40 nights.

The prosperity of desert people has usually depended on the proximity to water sources. Southern California's Imperial Valley, located in the Sonoran Desert has some of the world's richest farm land. But 90 years ago it was as dry and desolate as the desert areas that surround it. A combination of rich soil, unending sunshine and water diverted from the Colorado River first made it possible.

However, only a fraction of the desert lends itself to irrigation. In some deserts there is more oil than water, and the new colonizers are adventurers, not settlers.

My family lived close to the edge of town, and we loved to hike through the desert. Whether it was a lizard hunt with a slingshot, or a hike up a rocky mountain, we learned to appreciate and love the vast open land. We loved to hike across the desert to the Río Grande. Our adventures there were real and sometimes humorous.

Back in the fifties when car air conditioners were becoming popular, we drove through a 114-degree downtown El Paso in a lowered custom Ford with our windows rolled up, smiling and waving to sweltering people in the streets. We could do that for only a few minutes because we really didn't have an air conditioner.

At an earlier age, a Mexican gang of thugs on mules crossed the river to steal everything but our shirts. Another time Mexican kids crossed the river to steal my brother's tennis shoes. On the two-hour desert hike home we had to lend him one shoe or take turns carrying him.

Contrary to its original Latin translation, the desert is not "abandoned." It is not desolate. The desert is full of creatures that are invisible during the day, but come alive to feed at night.

Sunrises from the faraway mountain east of El Paso and the sunsets in New Mexico were breathtaking scenes unknown elsewhere. After a thunderstorm, the smell of wet desert brush carried a perfume of eternal memories. Close to home, the desert was safe enough to appreciate its danger and beauty.

C/S

My Ecumenical Father

¡Feliz Navidad! Merry Christmas! Happy Hanukkah! As a child, my season's greetings were tricultural—Mexicano, Anglo and Jewish.

Our devoutly Catholic parents raised three sons and three daughters in the basement of a Jewish synagogue, Congregation B'nai Zion in El Paso, Texas. José Cruz Burciaga was the custodian and *shabbat goy*. A shabbat goy is Yiddish for a Gentile who, on the Sabbath, performs certain tasks forbidden to Jews under orthodox law.

Every year around Christmas time, my father would take the menorah out and polish it. The eight-branched candleholder symbolizes Hanukkah, the commemoration of the first recorded war of liberation in that part of the world.

In 164 B.C., the Jewish nation rebelled against Antiochus IV Epiphanes, who had attempted to introduce pagan idols into the temples. When the temple was reconquered by the Jews, there was only one day's supply of oil for the Eternal Light in the temple. By a miracle, the oil lasted eight days.

My father was not only in charge of the menorah but for 40 years he also made sure the Eternal Light remained lit.

As children we were made aware of the differences and joys of Hanukkah, Christmas and Navidad. We were taught to respect each celebration, even if they conflicted. For example, the Christmas carols taught in school. We learned the song about the twelve days of Christmas, though I never understood what the hell a partridge was doing in a pear tree in the middle of December.

We also learned a German song about a boy named Tom and a bomb—*O Tannenbaum*. We even learned a song in the obscure language of Latin, called "Adeste Fideles," which reminded me of, *Ahh! d'este fideo,* a Mexican pasta soup. Though 75% of our class was Mexican-American, we never sang a Christmas song *en Español*. Spanish was forbidden.

So, our mother—a former teacher—taught us "Silent Night" in Spanish: *Noche de paz, noche de amor.* It was so much more poetic and inspirational.

While the rest of El Paso celebrated Christmas, Congregation B'Nai Zion celebrated Hanukkah. We picked up Yiddish and learned a Hebrew prayer of thanksgiving. My brothers and I would help my father hang the Hanukkah decorations.

At night, after the services, the whole family would rush across the border to Juarez and celebrate the *posadas,* which takes place for nine days before Christmas. They are a communal re-enactment of Joseph and Mary's search for shelter, just before Jesus was born.

To the posadas we took candles and candy left over from the Hanukkah celebrations. The next day we'd be back at St. Patrick's School singing, "I'm dreaming of a white Christmas."

One day I stopped dreaming of the white Christmases depicted on greeting cards. An old immigrant from Israel taught me Jesus was born in desert country just like that of the West Texas town of El Paso.

On Christmas Eve, my father would dress like Santa Claus and deliver gifts to his children, nephews, godchildren and the little kids in orphanages. The next day, minus his disguise, he would take us to Juárez, where we delivered gifts to the poor in the streets.

My father never forgot his childhood poverty and forever sought to help the less fortunate. He taught us to measure wealth not in money but in terms of love, spirit, charity and culture.

We were taught to respect the Jewish faith and culture. On the Day of Atonement, when the whole congregation fasted, my mother did not cook, lest the food odors distract. The respect was mutual. No one ever complained about the large picture of Jesus in our living room.

Through my father, leftover food from B'nai B'rith luncheons, Bar Mitzvahs and Bat Mitzvahs, found its way to Catholic or Baptist churches or orphanages. Floral arrangements in the temple that surrounded a Jewish wedding *hutpah* canopy many times found a second home at the altar of St. Patrick's Cathedral or San Juan Convent School. Surplus furniture, including old temple pews found their way to a missionary Baptist Church in *El Segundo Barrio*.

It was not uncommon to come home from school at lunch time and find an uncle priest, an aunt nun and a Baptist minister visiting our home at the same time that the Rabbi would knock on our door. It was just as natural to find the president of B'nai Zion eating beans and tortillas in our kitchen.

My father literally risked his life for the Jewish faith. Twice he was assaulted by burglars who broke in at night. Once he was stabbed in the hand. Another time he stayed up all night guarding the sacred Torahs after anti-semites threatened the congregation. He never philosophized about his ecumenism, he just lived it.

Cruz, as most called him, was a man of great humor, a hot temper and a passion for dance. He lived the Mexican Revolution and rode the rails during the Depression. One of his proudest moments came when he became a U.S. citizen.

September 23, 1985, sixteen months after my mother passed away, my father followed. Like his life, his death was also ecumenical. The funeral was held at Our Lady of Peace, where a priest said the mass in English. My cousins played mandolin and sang in Spanish. The president of B'nai Zion Congregation said a prayer in Hebrew. Members of the congregation sat with Catholics and Baptists.

Observing Jewish custom, the cortege passed by the synagogue one last time. Fittingly, father was laid to rest on the Sabbath. At the cemetery, in a very Mexican tradition, my brothers, sisters and I each kissed a handful of dirt and threw it on the casket.

I once had the opportunity to describe father's life to the late, great Jewish American writer Bernard Malamud. His only comment was, "Only in America!"

c/s

Tiburcio Vásquez:
A Chicano Perspective

Each southwestern state has several Mexican-American historical figures that in Anglo-American history are deemed outlaws, bandits or at best colorful folkloric figures from the old west. But to many Chicanos and Latin Americans, they were resisters and avengers.

Lesser known than Joaquin Murrieta or Gregorio Cortez is Tiburcio Vásquez from California. Early California journalists have left a wealth of information about this man.

Unfortunately, that wealth of details and facts covering the escapades, capture, trial and hanging of Tiburcio Vásquez does not fully explain the true nature of his long life outside gringo law.

To fully appreciate Tiburcio Vásquez the "outlaw," it is just as important to know his family genealogy, the social and political atmosphere in which he grew up, the ambivalent facts surrounding his first alleged crime, his reasons for running and how he eluded capture for so long.

Once these facts are taken into account, there is a reasonable conclusion that Tiburcio Vásquez was unlike other North American bandits of the old West, such as Billy the Kid or Jesse James. Their criminal lives were within their own social communities, and whatever their grudge against society, it was not based on injustices perpetrated by a conquering people.

Within the Mexican and Chicano communities, Tiburcio Vásquez has always been revered as an avenger. His place in Chicano history is not so much a colorful folkloric outlaw but as a Californio who refused to submit to the Yankee conquest.

Consider the family history that preceded Tiburcio Vásquez:

• In 1776, his grandfather, José Tiburcio Vásquez, with his wife and four children, rode with Juan Bautista de Anza to help found and settle the Presidio and *Misión de San Francisco*.

• In 1802, José Tiburcio Vásquez also helped found the new settlement of San Jose and became its first mayor.

• In 1831, the overland migration of Yankee settlers to California began with the Bartleson-Bidwell party.

• On August 11, 1835, the last Tiburcio Vásquez to become famous was born in Monterey, California.

Now consider the social and political climate in which he grew up:

• In 1836, the Texas revolution against Mexico broke out with the battle of the Alamo and concluded in San Jacinto, making Texas an independent republic that would exist under the Lone Star flag for ten years.

• In 1842, when Tiburcio was seven years old, Commodore Thomas Catesby Jones hoisted the U.S. flag over the peaceful settlement of Monterey and perplexed the Californio community. Jones had done this to foil a British flotilla steaming out of South America, which he feared was about to capture California. Jones was informed of his error, lowered the flag and sailed south to apologize to Governor Michetorrena. The event must have made a great impact on Tiburcio's impressionable young mind.

• In 1846, early Anglo-American pioneer Captain John C. Fremont supported the Yankee settlers in Northern California who were afraid that Colonel José Castro would expel them. With Fremont's approval, settlers Ezekiel Merritt, William B. Ide, Robert Semple, and others seized Colonel Mariano Vallejo, his brother Salvador, and brother-in-law Jacob Leese. Despite Vallejo's early kindness to the settlers, he and Salvador were jailed for two months at Sutter's Fort. That same year, when Tiburcio was eleven, the United States declared war on Mexico. Consider a quote from the *gobernador de California,* Pío Pico, who "hated the invading yankees with true Mexican cordiality." In his address to the state departmental assembly in May of that year, shortly before the Bear Flag Revolt, Pico stated:

"We find ourselves threatened by hordes of Yankee immigrants who have already begun to flock into our country and whose progress we cannot arrest. Already have wagons of that perfidious people scaled the most inaccessible summits of the Sierra Nevada, crossed the entire continent and penetrated the fruitful valley of Sacramento. What these astonishing people will next undertake I cannot say; but in whatever enterprize they embark they will be sure to be successful."

• In 1848, when Tiburcio was thirteen, the war ended with the signing of the Treaty of Guadalupe Hidalgo. Overnight, thousands of Mexicanos became citizens of a foreign government.

• In 1849, the gold rush brought Yankees by the hordes into California.

Young Tiburcio lived and witnessed this as he absorbed the words and feelings of parents, relatives and other Californio adults incensed over the intrusive Anglo-Americans. From a distinguished family, Tiburcio had been born into a California that was part of Mexico. From childhood to his teens, he had watched the massive influx of Yankees and had seen his people reduced to second-class citizens and worse.

In 1850, when Tiburcio was fifteen, California was admitted into the Union, and the Foreign Miners Tax severely penalized anyone but natural-born U.S. citizens mining for gold. This, even though early Californios had taught the Yankees how to pan for it.

By 1856, much of the land had changed to Yankee ownership through armed confrontations, legislation, and swindles as well as legitimate purchases. Lynchings of Mexicans became so common during the 1840s and 1850s that newspapers didn't even bother reporting them.

Those Californios who resisted the invading Yankee immigrants became outlaws. Professor Rodolfo Acuña,

California Chicano history professor and author of *Occupied America,* wrote:

"Resistance also manifested itself in anti-social behavior. When the colonized cannot earn a living within the system, or when they are degraded, they strike out. The most physical way is to rebel. This can be done in an organized way, as was done by Juan Cortina in Texas, or it can express itself in bandit activity. An analysis of the life of Tiburcio Vásquez clearly demonstrates that, while in the strict sense of the word he was a criminal, at the same time his underlying motivation was self-defense. Some Anglo-American folklorists have attempted to portray Tiburcio Vásquez as a comical and oversexed Mexican bandit. In stereotyping Vásquez, Anglos have purposely or unconsciously attempted to use satire to dismiss the legitimate grievance of Chicanos during the nineteenth century. While it is true that Tiburcio Vásquez was an outlaw, many Mexicans still consider him a hero."

Major Benjamin Truman, editor of *The Los Angeles Star,* interviewed Tiburcio some 22 years after the latter's first alleged crime. Vásquez's own perspective:

"My career grew out of the circumstances by which I was surrounded. As I grew into manhood I was in the habit of attending balls and parties given by the native Californians, into which the Americans, then beginning to become numerous, would force themselves and shove the native born men aside, monopolizing the dance and the women. This was about 1852. A spirit of hatred and revenge took possession of me. I had numerous fights in defense of what I believed to be my rights and those of my countrymen. The officers were continually in pursuit of me. I believed we were unjustly and wrongfully deprived of the social rights that belonged to us. So perpetually was I involved in these difficulties that at length I determined to leave the thickly settled portions of the country, and did so."

Tiburcio resented the Yankee sailors that swarmed over Monterey. He became proccupied with watching over his two sisters, guarding them against the aggressive and seemingly crude ways of a foreign culture.

Luis Valdez, director and founder of *El Teatro Campesino*, is an expert on Vásquez and proclaims him to be a precursor to the *pachuco* and the *cholo*. Valdez's theatrical play "Bandido" is about the life of Tiburcio Vásquez.

Tiburcio's first serious run-in with the law occurred in 1852, when he attended a dance with his friend Anastacio Garcia, who was married to Tiburcio's cousin, Guadalupe Gomez. Most Anglo-American historians have concluded, with no more evidence than hearsay, that Anastacio was a "bad hombre" who led Tiburcio astray. But Tiburcio's life tells us a different story: he was independent and more of a leader than a follower.

At the dance, Antonia Romero was dancing to a *son,* a favorite dance in which the men tossed their hats on the woman they liked as she danced by them. One young Yankee sailor decided to place his hat on Antonia Romero instead of flinging it. The young woman did not resist. A fight ensued.

Differing cultural customs can mean everything in such situations. While to "cut in" was perfectly normal conduct for a Yankee, to the Californio, it was an insult, a personal affront. "Cutting in" is still considered a dangerous practice in many parts of the Southwest, Mexico and Latin America. Machismo is not necessarily the negative Anglo-

American interpretation. To a Latino male, machismo can also be an honest self-assurance to defend country, women and honor with their very life.

In any case, when the fight ensued, Constable Hardimount was called to quell the disturbance. When he appeared on the scene and began to question the people in attendance, someone turned off the lamps. By the time they were relit, the constable was dead.

Implicated in the fight were José Guerra, Anastacio García and Tiburcio Vásquez.

José Guerra was lynched the morning after the murder without a trial. Vásquez and García escaped but a few months later, Garcia was apprehended in Los Angeles and returned to Monterey for trial. But the trial never took place because outraged vigilantes found out, raided the jail and immediately lynched him.

Tiburcio Vásquez did what any red-blooded Californio of that time would have done under those circumstances. Because due process in an Anglo-American court of justice seemed impossible, he decided that it would be better to live outside the Yankee law of the day. To have decided otherwise would have been suicidal.

Tiburcio's decision to run and live outside of the Anglo-American dominated society was doubtlessly affected by what Tiburcio, in his young lifetime, had witnessed of Yankee atrocities, thefts and vigilante-style lynchings. While one wrong does not justify another injustice, these circumstances cast him more in the light of a rebel and avenger than a common criminal.

After begining his life as an outlaw, Tiburcio went to his mother and told her that he intended to commence a different life. "I asked for and obtained her blessing and at once commenced the career of a robber." Thus did Tiburcio Vásquez become a hunted criminal.

Tiburcio Vásquez further stated, "I had confederates with me from the first and was always recognized as a leader." Also, according to him, his life as a robber was fast-paced and his robberies numerous until his arrest in 1857 or 1858 for horse stealing in Los Angeles. He was sent to San Quentin.

In 1859, Vásquez participated in a prison break but was soon captured. In prison he was active in stirring up revolts among the inmates. Released in 1863, Tiburcio resumed his bandido life.

Despite intense and costly searches across the state, Vásquez always eluded capture. One comment from that time explains why:

"All of these people (Mexican) are his attached friends, offer him the shelter of their houses when he is pursued and tell the officers the most prodigious lies without any compunction.

"He has no band or gang, unless the entire Mexican population of the mountain regions of Fresno, Kern, Tulare, Monterey and Los Angeles counties can be called such."

In all of these counties, Vásquez could count on the moral and physical support of his countrymen—and according to many, his countrywomen. Many romantic escapades are attributed to Tiburcio Vásquez. Some credence must be given to many of these episodes, considering the nature of Tiburcio's life on the run, as well as documented occurrences. At his last trial, nine out of every ten spectators were women.

Tiburcio often risked capture to visit a woman friend. One time he supposedly made his escape by dressing in women's clothes.

Despite his general support among the Spanish-speaking populace, Tiburcio was not without Californio enemies—sometimes created by his romantic escapades. Such was the case with Abdón Leiva. Tiburcio was smitten by the charms of Abdón's wife, Rosaria. Abdón supposedly discovered them in *flagrante delicto* and aided in the capture of Tiburcio. Abdón testified against Tiburcio at his last trial.

Though his attraction to the ladies sometimes landed him in costly indiscretions, Tiburcio Vásquez was otherwise prudent, intelligent, resourceful and commanding. Many times, when traveling, he would have one companion ride far ahead of him and another far behind to warn him of any dangers. And when camping, Tiburcio normally chose to sleep away from the main campsite.

Another favored tactic when holding up a stagecoach was for Tiburcio and his men to form a single file on horseback so as to appear as one horseman to the drivers of the stage coach. At the last moment, the bandidos would spread out and surprise their intended prey.

According to Stanford University history professor Albert Camarillo, "Vásquez created fear in the Anglos because of his revolutionary potential. Tiburcio, on at least one occasion, had ambitions of affecting an uprising or revolution against the 'Yankee invaders of California.' He stated that 'Given $60,000 dollars, I would be able to recruit enough arms and men to revolutionize Southern California.' Indeed, Tiburcio Vásquez was able to free himself of the Anglo colonization and become a 'quasi-bandit revolutionary'." In fact, to the end, Vásquez had hoped that before hanging he would have a chance to make a speech on the scaffold, calling for a revolution.

Perhaps, Tiburcio's would have been an ill-fated revolution, considering the numbers and dominance of the Yankee invaders. But other revolutions have been enhanced by so-called "outlaws." Pancho Villa and Emiliano Zapata were long labelled bandits, murderers, plunderers and rapists. They came from the oppressed classes. Today, Elfego Baca from New Mexico, Juan Cortina and Gregorio Cortez from Texas would have been called terrorists.

Tiburcio Vásquez was eventually captured after he was betrayed by Abdón Leiva in a secret operation. Following a lengthy trial and much publicity, Vásquez was hung at 30 minutes past one on the afternoon of March 19, 1875. Fourteen minutes later he was declared dead.

C/s

Ernesto Galarza 1905–1984

"I'm calling to tell you Ernesto has left us. Please tell those people who loved and cared for him ..."

With those calm and resigned words of grief, Mae Galarza notified Cecilia and I of Ernesto's passing on the morning of June 22 in their San Jose home. Their beautiful marriage of 55 years had finally come to an end. He also left two daughters, Karla and Eliu. "He was tired," said Mae. "He worked since he was five years old." Ernesto was 78.

Those people who loved and cared for him extended far beyond his immediate family to those he never met. Ernesto Galarza, a sort of dean of Chicano educators and activists, was loved and admired by people everywhere, but by Chicanos especially, for it was this pioneer who inspired us through his legacy and writing. In the sixties, when Chicanos fought for social justice in the fields, barrios, and classrooms, he seemed to be the only model we had. We read *Barrio Boy* and *Tragedy at Chualar.* He spoke and wrote with authority and authenticity, two elements we so painfully lacked then.

His accomplishments are too many, his awards too numerous to list, and they overshadow the person that he was—quiet and unassuming, yet articulate and outspoken.

In 1943 he received Bolivia's highest honor, the Award of the Condor, for his work with organized labor there. And a few years ago, he still found time to help save Alviso, a poor barrio just outside of San Jose, from being converted into a dump site.

Galarza organized and championed the causes of farmworkers when Cesar Chavez was still a youngster. His book, *Merchants of Labor,* was the first authoritative and crisp analysis of the *bracero* program. He wrote about the thousands of Mexican laborers who came to "lend an arm" to the agribusiness of the Southwest. He spoke with conviction and compassion about the injustices they suffered.

To us Galarza was a giant. We had read his work as college students. My wife, Cecilia, was fortunate to have been loaned a carbon copy of *Merchants of Labor* in 1963. In 1972, Stanford University acquired the complete collection of Galarza's farm labor research.

In a speech presented at San Jose State University, December 19, 1973, Ernest Galarza spoke on the Chicano Experience. No one has ever expressed more eloquently what a Chicano is.

"I call him Chicano, in the first place, because that is

what he wishes to be called, and respect for self-identity is a universal right. I call him a Chicano because he is a historical presence within an ethnic minority that is already different because of him. He is, furthermore, a Chicano because of his posture in which belligerence, a particular quality of social awareness, a distinct kind of romanticism, are unmistakable. There is also a Chicano style which cannot be mistaken for that of any other in American society today. If in some important respects his passion is pledged to a dream of Aztlán, he can and does argue that at least his is a passionate style of life. Feeling robbed of an ancestral cultural endowment he currently lives and acts according to symbols that outrage his detractors much more than they subdue their arrogance or reduce their power.

"But these Chicanos are not the first social beings to be driven to passion by their past in order to contend with the realities of their present. When the wells of emotion are filled only by resentment, a crying sense of injustice, racist affronts, deliberately designed frustrations to personal development and social worthiness, it may be suspect that the gods are making mad those they would destroy—the gods of power whose safety depends upon keeping the despairs of their various minorities apart. This, I think, is where the Chicano currently stands."

We have vivid memories of meeting Galarza for the first time. We were in awe of him at first, but Galarza had that quality of a truly great person—he asked about our work in art, writing and education. He listened to the voices in the Chicano community—workers and professionals— and thoughtfully pondered what he had heard. He had long ago discovered that there were no easy answers to the complex and diverse nature of our communities. He became a mentor to hundreds of Chicanos who all wanted his guidance. And Galarza found time to give that most precious of commodities to them: time and individual attention.

He spoke with legitimacy. He was educated through a B.A. from Occidental, an M.A. from Stanford and a Ph.D. in political science from Columbia University. He spoke with authority because he had lived the life of a farmworker before his educational accomplishments led him to work as a consultant to OEO/Whitney and the Ford Foundation.

Galarza inspired joy. He looked at each day with a sense of renewed energy and he never lost his sense of wonder— that quality we so often lose as adults conquered by daily routine.

We will always hold dear a luncheon invitation we received from Mae and Ernesto. We sat at their table along with our two children. Their home was serene and we were typical nervous parents with a six-year-old and toddler, hoping they wouldn't touch or break anything. Mae and Ernesto opened their home and hearts to all four of us. Both of them focused on the children. They showed us their garden, which had provided virtually everything they had served for lunch. Galarza spoke about a peach tree as one would talk about an old friend. The tree was now old and no longer bountiful, but the Galarzas had decided to let it preside over their garden until it decided to wither away on its own.

He gave us a collection of his children's books for our own. They are a poetic treasure of Mexican childhood rhymes. We sensed he had immensely enjoyed writing them.

A month-and-a-half before his death, Galarza was invited to speak before a group of Chicano graduates from Gilroy, California. He had to decline due to his poor health. The Gilroy committee then decided to invite Cecilia and I to serve as keynote speakers. It was ironic. He went away on that day of celebration for the precious young Gilroy high school and community college graduates. At that time only 40 percent of the Chicano students in that town received a high school diploma.

At that reunion, we paused for a moment of prayer in memory of Ernesto Galarza, friend and inspiration to so many of us. We also remembered another great writer and educator, friend, and colleague, Tomás Rivera, the late chancellor of the University of California at Riverside.

They were sad and trying times for Chicanos everywhere, having lost two great writers and educators, two friends, in the span of five weeks. We faced challenges that seemed overwhelming: the Simpson-Mazzoli Immigration Bill, a Supreme Court decision on affirmative action, the threat against bilingual education and bilingual ballots. These were causes Galarza had championed.

He encouraged me as a writer. We exchanged poems. From his poetry book *Kodachromes in Rhyme,* we found a verse that gave strength and comfort:

I only sang
Because the lonely road was long;
and now the road and I are gone
but not the song ...

C/s

133

The First Chicano Actor Hired By Luis Valdéz

On the same day Lucille Ball died, another great but lesser-known comedian passed away. Felipe Cantú, who worked most of his life as a poor *campesino,* was one of the first actors of *El Teatro Campesino* and founder of the *Teatro Chicano* style of acting. The founder of El Teatro Campesino, Luis Valdéz, recalled "He combined the styles of Brecht and Cantinflas."

Felipe Cantú was born August 23, 1921 in Atongo del Bajo, Nuevo León, Mexico and passed away April 26, 1989 in Bakersfield, California.

It was mid-December, 1965, in a Delano field when 44-year-old Felipe Cantú crossed a United Farm Worker picket line to work as a pruner, not so much for the *patrón,* as for his *familia.* With Christmas around the corner

Felipe was not about to turn down a job. He had a wife and seven young mouths to feed.

As he pruned the grape vines, UFW organizers lined the field yelling in spanish, "Join *la huelga, compañero!*" He yelled back, joked and laughed with the strikers. They not only spoke the same language, they knew the same struggle, the same migration, from one field to the next, one crop to the next, one pain to the next.

When he came to the end of the row, Felipe stopped pruning and continued talking and joking. Then, as if he had been with the strikers the whole afternoon, he walked away from his job and joined the UFW. He looked strange with one crooked eye and the ear flaps of an aviator's cap ready to fly away. Luis Valdez studied him and thought, "Who *is* this guy?"

The next day Luis Valdéz and Agustín Lira recruited him for the newly formed Teatro Campesino. He was a natural, complete with stage presence and the ability to project beyond crowded meeting rooms and flat-bed trucks.

Felipe became the prototype of El Teatro Campesino. Valdez gives him a lot of credit, "A lot of people don't realize the impact of one campesino." Felipe established a level of performance that influenced the whole Chicano Theater movement. Many of the techniques the teatro learned on the road were assimilated by osmosis from Felipe." He had picked these up working as a clown, a *payaso* in the Mexican *carpa* tradition, tent performances. Valdéz recalls that his expressions and natural use of his body as incredible.

Felipe had a unique, classy face, diamond in shape, broad at the top and tapered to a sharp chin. Felipe could make you laugh or make you cry. He drew from his experiences. He went through life collecting and inventing jokes, stories, expressions. "Typically campesino! Stone campesino!" Luis recalled.

In the begining the campesinos were given free reign on stage. Felipe took the ball, ran, and never stopped. Beyond clowning he would go into real dramatic moments. If there ever was a farmworker actor mold for Chicano theater, it was Felipe Cantú.

"He had one crooked eye and I think that's what led to his being funny," recalls Luis Valdéz. In 1967, the Farmworkers Clinic took him to Stanford Hospital for corrective surgery. "That's one of the really touching moments that I'll never forget", recalled Valdéz. "After the operation we brought him home to Delano, a little *casita,* a shack. His kids and wife came out and they were all crying, holding his face, looking at his eyes. They couldn't get over the fact that he was looking straight now. It changed him but not his humor. It gave him an added sense of dignity."

Those were the happy early days of El Teatro Campesino. Amid ragged props and children spilling onto the stage, Felipe and the campesino actors created impromptu *actos* with one goal in mind—*la huelga.* Felipe's little boys reveled in watching their father perform.

In the begining, the characters in the plays wore cardboard signs with their roles as campesinos, patrones, *huelguistas* or *esquiroles.* During one performance, Felipe was wearing a sign that said, *Don Sotaco,* small man. Suddenly, his sign fell off and Felipe came to a dead frozen stop. Then he gently bent down to pick up his sign as if he had lost his identity. "Everybody cracked up. It was a powerful moment. He was funny on stage, he was funny off stage."

The 1967 Teatro Campesino national tour is a road of memories filled with anecdotes about Felipe el payaso. Felipe the clown.

There was the time at Reed College in Oregon. Luis was giving a serious talk to students and faculty when he heard his name whispered from behind a flap of the curtain only he could see. Luis turned to discover Felipe with his pants around his ankles. It took everything to keep Luis from breaking up with laughter.

On a tour to the Northwest, Felipe drank too much one night and turned sentimental. Hanging on to Luis, Felipe told him, "I love you, *cabrón?* Because you're like my father!" Luis recalls, "Here I was, 26 and Felipe was 48. He considered himself one of the boys. Inside he was six years old." But the compliment between two friends was sincere from the founder of Teatro Chicano style of acting to the father of El Teatro Campesino.

Felipe loved to sing and compose songs. On the march to Sacramento in '66 he composed a *corrido* to Cesar Chavez and every time they stopped at a different town he added a new verse and the song kept getting longer and longer. "It's a good thing we got to Sacramento," Luis told Felipe, "otherwise this corrido would be unsingable.

Another time they traveled to San Antonio where they stopped to eat at the Mi Tierra restaurant. Felipe recognized the restaurant, "I used to come here all the time and eat free. I'm going to show you how I used to do it. You go in, sit down and watch." So the whole *tropa* of actors walked in, took a table, sat down, and waited, watching the entrance. Felipe staggered in, disheveled, disoriented, and shaking like a *loco*, looking around, staring at the waitress and throwing a glance at his *compañeros*. The waitress took compassion on the poor trembling man, walked over, gently took his arm and said, "Let me sit you here." Then she brought him a free bowl of *posole*. When everyone met outside afterwards, Felipe cracked up, "Didn't I tell you?" He loved to perform and act in real life.

He was given to funny impromptu speeches in Spanish to everyone and to no one. "Compañeros!" He would say, "Los Patrones are against us! But, *Nosotros! Nosotros!*" then he would begin to softly sing the love song *Nosotros Que Fuimos Tan Sinceros* ... and do a little *bolero* dance.

His comedy was beyond Chaplin or Cantinflas for it was born from the deepest essence of humor, which is pain— something he knew so well all the way to the end.

Felipe was amazed at the things he saw. He was amazed to visit the nation's capital. In Washington, D.C. Teatro was invited to a party at the Watergate Hotel given by Hubert Humphrey. Many notable politicians attended. Felipe went around taking pictures.

At the Newport Folk Festival in '67, El Teatro Campesino was on stage with Joan Baez, Judy Collins, Buffy St. Marie, Arlo Guthrie and Bob Dylan. At a party afterward Felipe went to the one person that could understand him in Spanish—Joan Baez. Felipe liked her right away and asked Luis, *"Quien es esta chava?"*—"Who's this chick?" Then he met her bilingual parents and got along great with them.

If Felipe had delusions of grandeur he always had a sense of charm, never with conceit. The people found him loveable and he enjoyed the attention.

He loved people. He was a passionate yet a gentle man. Instead of swearing with a "God ..." he would change it to *"gatos güeros!"* and had everybody saying it. He disliked stubborness in people and called them "burros without a master."

In 1967 their national tour ended with El Teatro Campesino and the United Farm Workers amiably separating. Felipe was caught in the middle. He was torn between his love for acting and the reality that he needed the UFW to feed his family. But his love for his familia always came first. Genoveva, his young wife, suffered from epileptic seizures all her life and he never failed to provide for her.

Felipe bid farewell to acting, but not for long. A year later he returned to El Teatro Campesino in Del Rey, California. But his dreams were short lived after a couple of performances. He realized El Teatro could not even afford to pay the rent. "It was painful," Luis remembered. Felipe went back to Bakersfield, minus the UFW and his acting carreer.

During his remaining years Felipe returned to El Teatro Campesino for sporadic performances and, in 1987 acted in Luis Valdez's award-winning PBS Special, *Corridos*, with Linda Ronstadt.

His role as a *curandero,* a folk healer in the film *La Bamba* was more reality than fiction. "You're talking down poverty," explains Valdéz. That small role was a crown on a career that began from the day he walked away from the field to join a strike.

Felipe was already frail and ill when he filmed *Corridos* and *La Bamba*. One of Luis Valdez's favorite moments in *La Bamba* is when Felipe twinkles a smile at Ritchie Valens, knowing the young singer's fate. Felipe's role in that hit film gave him a renewed sense of dignity and importance among his friends and Bakersfield neighbors.

Towards the end Felipe lost his speech from cancer of the throat. He had been a heavy smoker. As he was being prepared to have his windpipe removed in an operation, he could barely talk but he joked in spanish, "They're taking me to *la chi .. chi ...*" then he cracked up for he could no longer say the word.

His old friend Augie noted the irony, "He couldn't speak but Felipe really didn't need his voice. He was able to communicate through his body, face, and movements. And when he did talk he had a patter a mile a minute and we laughed whether we understood or not."

Felipe Cantú had a genius comparable to that of Chaplin and Cantinflas, as I have said. The only difference is that the guy never really had a chance to flower except in Teatro where he laid down the foundation for the whole Teatro Campesino style. "His mannerisms might have been *puro Nuevo León* or Texas, but he was universal," said Valdéz.

On his deathbed he was surrounded by the loving presence of his children Miguel, Linda, Meme, Blanca, Lupe and Nuno. Their mother, Genoveva, whom Felipe had gently loved for so many years had died five years earlier. Another son José Luis was killed in the streets of Los Angeles. Another is serving time in prison for murder. Miguel the eldest continues in the campesino tradition.

It is significant that Felipe died on the same day as Lucille Ball. Luis Valdéz puts him right up there with her. "The only difference is that this guy never got the chance to shine. His story is like the story of so many. How many people like Felipe have come and gone? I see a universal thread. This is just one that managed to get a little bit of attention. But he left his impact. Through his improv and his sense of humor, he helped set up a whole comical tone in Chicano Theater."

On Friday morning April 28, 1989, Felipe Cantú was laid to rest in the San Joaquín soil he had toiled in for so many years. Luis and his wife Lupe were present. Rogelio Rojas, a second generation Teatro Campesino actor, traveled overnight from San Juán Bautista to bid farewell to his *Maestro*. "It's ironic," said Rogelio, "the day he was buried, a third generation of Teatro Campesino actors began their play, *El Fín Del Mundo*"—"The End of the World."

C/s

A Magazine For the Dead

Life has to be the most popular magazine of all time in this country. Through vibrant photographs in living color and dramatic black and white, it celebrates life in this country. But to some extent, all magazines are filled with life and the present time, begining with *Time, Newsweek,* and *People.* There are magazines for all occasions—from walking to war to collecting hangnails. But there is no magazine for the Dead.

And so I would like to propose a national magazine about death. Death is big business in this country. Everybody has to die sometime, some way, somehow, but it's such a hush-hush subject. Why should morticians, embalmers, cemeteries, casket-makers, grave-diggers, cremators and flower shops monopolize the industry? Death is not a dead-end road. There is a lot of money in death. Some people would consider such a publication in bad taste. But I've never seen bad taste stop anyone from making money in this country. Look at the fast food business.

Moral, social, psychological and economic causes would be well served by such a periodical. It has gotten so expensive to die that many people hesitate to do it because of the expense alone.

Death is constantly hidden from us. There is a daily list of obituaries, but it is usually hidden just before the classified section or in the second-to-the-last page of some obscure section. Unless you are *somebody,* obituaries contain very little information. Only if the person was famous will their death make headlines.

At least one national or international celebrity dies every week. There should be a cover story on not only her or his contributions but also their lifestyle and type of death. Obituary readers are often left wondering if the person smoked, died from drugs, cholesterol or boredom.

Some corporations would find it appropriate to advertise in such a magazine, especially the alcohol, tobacco, automobile, chemical, and weapons industry. The Marines, Army and Navy could advertise: "Join up and see the other world! Be all that you can be!" or "We need a few good dead men!" The profits to be reaped from these grim reapers have not been totally tapped. A classified section could list other little-known deaths around the country to help people look for long-lost relatives, inheritors or inheritances.

There are many people who experience death and remember hovering over their own bodies, speeding down a tunnel, seeing the light at the end and reaching the clouded dunes of heaven only to be turned back like a bad dream, like picking a monopoly game card that says, "Go back to earth. You owe the hospital $10,000."

A classified section could carry requests from living donors looking for body parts or rare blood types. Article ideas are endless: how to have the perfect funeral; ten tips for frugal funerals; choosing the perfect casket; color caskets to match your personality; what to put on your tombstone; prevent getting ripped off when a loved one dies; and a horoscope for the dead.

There could be a recipe section: Ten easy recipes for the grieving and bereaved. *Pan de muerto,* bread of the dead, is a delicious Mexican pastry. Mexican candy skulls made from sugar are also very popular during Mexico's Day of the Dead.

Mexico is a gold mine of information about death. If the United States has a fascination with life, so does Mexico— but it is balanced by a fascination or obsession with death.

Our next-door neighbor has been honoring the faithful dead since before the conquest. Their holiday, *El Día de los Muertos,* sounds just as scary in English if uttered in a soft guttural voice, "The Day of the Dead!" The Aztecs celebrated a whole month for the dead and by coincidence ended on All Souls Day. The Spanish conquerors tried to do away with the month-long celebration by celebrating All Souls day, but the dead seem to be winning over the saints.

There have been several magazines about death in Mexico but they have been one-time educational or humorous publications without the capitalist ideas suggested here. Each year for the Day of the Dead, Mexican newspapers publish epitaphs and obituaries for still-living politicians, business people and other well-known personas. Half in jest, on that day alone, journalists and artists can rake their favorite or least-favorite *politico* over red-hot coals in rhyme and with or without reason.

Awareness and celebration of El Día de los Muertos in this country is greater each year not only with the Indo-Hispanic population but with the mainstream popular culture.

Should you be interested in starting up such a magazine, remember where you read it. I have the copyright, 1992.

C/s